Howard Zinn
on
History

Howard Zinn on History

Howard Zinn

SEVEN STORIES PRESS
New York • London • Sydney • Toronto

Seven Stories Press
140 Watts Street
New York, NY 10013
www.sevenstories.com

In Canada:
Publishers Group Canada, 250A Carlton Street, Toronto, ON M5A 2L1

In the U.K.:
Turnaround Publisher Services Ltd., Unit 3, Olympia Trading Estate, Coburg Road, Wood Green, London N22 6TZ

In Australia: Palgrave Macmillan, 627 Chapel Street, South Yarra, VIC 3141

Library of Congress Cataloging-in-Publication Data

Zinn, Howard, 1922–
Howard Zinn on history / Howard Zinn.
p.   cm.
ISBN 1-58322-048-8 (pbk.) / ISBN-13 978-1-58322-048-1
1. Zinn, Howard, 1922–   —Political and social views. 2. History, Modern—Philosophy.
3. United States—Politics and government—Philosophy. I. Title.
D16.9.Z57 2000   00-032959
901—dc21

9 8 7 6 5 4 3 2

College professors may order examination copies of Seven Stories Press titles for a free six-month trial period. To order, visit www.sevenstories.com/textbook, or fax on school letterhead to (212) 226-1411.

Printed in Canada.

Contents

VI. Portraits

PART 1

On Activism

1

Words
of
Encouragement

The following essay was written after I attended an international gathering of socialists in London, and reflected on the degree of pessimism we find among people on the Left these days.

The order came from above (I will not reveal the name, unless tortured): "Write something inspirational." The exact words were: "Inspire, please." The courteous approach concealed a certain desperation. For those not in the know, let me explain that we who write for the progressive-radical movement have our specialties. Some specialize in writing depressing stuff. Others write humorous pieces. Some concentrate on trashing other Left writers. It seems that there was an opening this month for someone to inspire, and I was chosen.

Not an easy job, when the United States government (I was about to say "we," in Dan Rather style, but decided that my interests and those of the White House do not coincide) has just finished dropping thousands of cluster bombs on Yugoslavia, the victims being whoever happened to be in the vicinity, whether Albanians or Serbs, men or women, adults or children, who are now dead, or without limbs. And yet my editor says: "Inspire, please."

Okay, let me have a go at it. I've just returned from London, where I was invited to speak to a gathering of socialists (I won't get more specific than that) who assemble every year, I learned, around the topic of "Marxism." I confess that what enticed me was that they promised to do a one-evening performance of my play "Marx in Soho," a one-person play in which Marx appears in the present, saying, with a laugh (yes, Marx really said this to someone who annoyed him): "I'm not a Marxist!"

Well (to get away from promoting my play, though it's hard), I expected to find assembled in London a few hundred aging, solemn Leftists who, against the general insistence, across the political spectrum, that "Marxism is dead," insist on the importance of the old "Moor" and the validity of the socialist ideal.

I had the numbers wrong. Not hundreds, but six thousand were there, mostly from the United Kingdom, many from other European countries, and some from the United States. I also had the ages wrong. They were almost all young people, from early twenties to early thirties. And I had the temperament wrong. They were lively, exuberant, fun-loving people.

Maybe you won't agree, but I found this inspiring. Or, to use less extravagant language, encouraging. Six thousand people, assembled in one place, who believe in socialism, and who were denouncing the actions of the U.S. and Britain in Yugoslavia? At a time when the British Labour Party, once committed to socialism, is Blairing forth its belief in the wonders of the market, and the miracle of bombing? Yes, that's encouraging.

Now comes the difficult part. The gathering was sponsored by the Socialist Workers Party. Yes, as some on the Left would say, caustically, "the Trots."

And about half of the six thousand people seemed to be trying to sell the Party newspaper, the Socialist Worker, to the other half. I have always been careless about security matters, and, have never checked the credentials, or run their literature through a scanner, of people or organizations who invited me to speak to them. I suppose I have been so hungry for listeners that, unlike Groucho Marx, I will talk to any group that will have me.

I recall a moment during the Vietnam War when a self-appointed political commissar of the anti-war movement phoned me: "Howard, I see you endorsed the anti-war rally called by the SWP [yes, that same inescapable bunch]. You really should have run that by me." Well, I was always repelled by this scrutinizing of people who, whatever they were doing at other times, seemed to be devoting themselves at the moment to a worthy cause. As sectarians often say, let's not be sectarian.

The London conference began with a spirited rally at the Friends Meeting House (those Quakers don't scrutinize either, the softies!) at which Tariq Ali, the veteran English radical, subjected the New Labour honchos now ruling Britain to an eloquent and scathing critique. And the next days were filled with dozens and dozens of gatherings, with these young, eager people rushing from one to another, whether the subjects were topical (East Timor, global warming, Kosovo, blues and rock, the arms trade) or theoretical ("the birth of historical materialism," "is there progress in history"), or esoteric political economy ("the labor theory of value," "the declining rate of profit").

It was encouraging to find people there who foreshadow a coming multiracial generation of radicals. Like the young woman, born in Vietnam, transported to the United States at the age of two by her parents. Her father had been in the Saigon army and a supporter of the United States, but over the years his daughter, now an enthusiastic socialist, had led him to rethink his views.

The evenings were filled with music, disco, plays. And movies: Kubrick's *Full Metal Jacket* (Vietnam at its rawest), *Gallipoli* (one of the most powerful of anti-war films), *When We Were Kings* (Muhammad Ali).

It was not a gathering of scholars but of activists. And so the air was filled with leaflets advertising this or that rally, demonstration, action.

There was no coverage in the mainstream English press: not in the *Times*, the *Guardian*, the *Independent*. Which should instruct us all, not to judge the degree of dissidence in the society by what we see in the media. Imagine how many gatherings and actions are taking place all the time that we don't know about because they are not covered by radio, television, or newspapers.

But when you look closely, when you listen to alternative radio broadcasting, read outside-the-mainstream periodicals (*The Progressive, Z Magazine, The Nation, In These Times*), check the stories in *The Nuclear Resister,* or the newsletters put out by Jonah House in Baltimore, keep your eyes open for unorthodox sources of information, secretly check the internet—you realize how many people in this country and all over the world do not accept the political and economic system that now dominates.

I don't know about you, but I am encouraged.

2

Seattle:
A Flash
of the Possible

In December, 1999, an electrifying event, flashed on television screens around the country, was brought to the attention of the entire nation—tens of thousands of people assembled in Seattle, Washington, protesting the policies of the World Bank and the International Monetary Fund. I thought it was a historic moment, and wrote about it as follows.

In the year 1919, when the city of Seattle was brought to a halt by a general strike—beginning with 35,000 shipyard workers demanding a wage increase—the mayor reflected on its significance:

True there were no flashing guns, no bombs, no killings. Revolution...doesn't need violence. The general strike, as practiced in Seattle, is of itself the weapon of revolution, all the more dangerous because quiet. To succeed it must suspend everything; stop the entire life stream of a community....That is to say, it puts the government out of operation. And that is all there is to revolt—no matter how achieved.

What happened in Seattle recently was not as large an event as the general strike of 1919, but it suggested, as that did, how apparently powerless people, if they unite in large numbers, can bring the machinery of government and commerce to a halt. In an era when the power of government, and of multi-national corporations, is overwhelming, it is instructive to get even a hint of how fragile that power is when confronted by organized, determined citizens.

When the civil rights activists of the South in the early Sixties put into practice the principle they called "Nonviolent Direct Action," they were able to make heretofore invincible power yield. What happened recently in Seattle was another working out of that principle. Whatever the substance of the Seattle protests, they revealed, as happens at certain times in the history of societies, how vulnerable are the holders of power when people unite in large numbers for a common cause.

We must acknowledge that many of us, even veterans of social movements of the past, have begun to feel helpless as we observed the frightening consolidation of control, the giant corporations merging, the American military machine grown to monstrous proportions. But we were forgetting certain fundamental facts about power: that the most formidable military machine depends ultimately on the obedience of its soldiers, that the most powerful corporation becomes helpless when its workers stop working, when its customers refuse to buy its products.

The strike, the boycott, the refusal to serve, the ability to paralyze the functioning of a complex social structure—these remain potent weapons against the most fearsome state or corporate power. Note how General Motors and Ford had to surrender to the strikers of the Thirties, how black children marching in Birmingham in 1963 pushed Congress into passing a Civil Rights Act, how the U.S. government, carrying on a war in Vietnam had to reconsider in the face of draft resistance and desertions en masse, how a garbage workers strike in New York immobilized a great city, how the threat of a boycott against Texaco for racist policies brought immediate concessions.

The Seattle protests, even if only a microcosm of future situations, even if only a gleam of possibility in the disheartening dark of our time, should cause us to recall basic principles of power and powerlessness, so easily forgotten as the flood of media nonsense washes over the history of social movements.

It has been discouraging to watch the control of information in this county get tighter and tighter as megacorporations have taken over television and radio stations, newspapers, even book publishing. And yet, we saw in Seattle that when tens of thousands of men and women fill the streets and halt the normal flow of business and government, and march with colorful banners and giant puppets and an infectious enthusiasm, they could break through the barriers of the corporate media and excite the attention of people all over the country, and around the world.

Of course, the television cameras rushed to cover the fires (set actually by exploding tear gas bombs) and broken windows. The term "anarchist" was used to describe the perpetrators, by journalists ignorant—as were the window-smashers themselves—of the philosophy of anarchism. But it was not lost on viewers that the vast majority of people marching through the streets were angry, even obstructive, but peaceful—yes, non-violent direct action.

In Seattle, the demonstrators were grappling with economic issues impossibly complex—globalization, protectionism, export trade, intellectual properties—issues the most sophisticated experts have had a hard time explaining. But through all of that complexity, a certain diamond-hard idea shone through: that the schemes of well-dressed men of finance and government gathering in ornate halls were dangerous to the health and lives of working people all over the world. And that thousands in the streets, representing millions, were determined to resist.

In one crucial way, it was a turning point in the history of the movements of recent decades—a departure from the single-issue focus of the Seabrook occupation of 1977, the nuclear-freeze gathering in

Central Park in 1982, the great Washington events of the Million-Man March, the Stand for Children, the parade of women. This time, the union movement was at the center. The issue of class—rich and poor, here and all over the globe—bound everyone together.

It was at the least, a flash of the possible. It recalled the prophecy of A. Philip Randolph in November of 1963, speaking to an AFL-CIO convention shortly after the civil rights March on Washington of 200,000 people, black and white. Randolph told the delegates: "The Negro's protest today is but the first rumbling of the under-class. As the Negro has taken to the streets, so will the unemployed of all races take to the streets."

There will undoubtedly be more rumblings, with more people of color involved, of unemployed and employed, men and women. Seattle was a good sign.

3

The Optimism
of Uncertainty

The word "optimism," used here, makes me a little uneasy, because it suggests a blithe, slightly sappy whistler in the dark of our time. But I use it anyway, not because I am totally confident that the world will get better, but because I am certain that *only* such confidence can prevent people from giving up the game before all the cards have been played. The metaphor is deliberate; it is a gamble. Not to play is to foreclose any chance of winning. To play, to act, is to create at least a possibility of changing the world. I wrote about this in a much longer piece requested by John Tirman of the Winston Foundation, and this essay appeared in my book *Failure to Quit* (Common Courage Press, 1993).

As this century draws to a close, a century packed with history, what leaps out from that history is its utter unpredictability.

This confounds us, because we are talking about exactly the period when human beings became so ingenious technologically that they could plan and predict the exact time of someone landing on the moon.

But who foresaw that, twenty-four years after the national Democratic Party Convention refused to seat blacks from Mississippi, a black militant would run for president, excite crowds, black and white, all over the country, and then dominate the Democratic Party Convention in Atlanta? Or (recalling Jesse Jackson's presentation of Rosa Parks to the Convention) who, on that day in Montgomery, Alabama, in 1955, when Rose Parks refused to move from the front of the bus, could have predicted that this would lead to a mass protest of black working people, and then would follow a chain of events that would shake the nation, startle the world, and transform the South?

But let's go back to the turn of the century. That a revolution should overthrow the Tsar of Russia, in that most sluggish of semi-feudal empires, not only startled the most advanced imperial powers, but took Lenin himself by surprise and sent him rushing by train to Petrograd.

Who could have predicted, not just the Russian Revolution, but Stalin's deformation of it, then Khrushchev's astounding exposure of Stalin, and recently Gorbachev's succession of surprises?

Or observe Germany after the first World War. There was a situation that fitted the Marxist model of social revolution most neatly— an advanced industrial society, with an educated, organized proletariat, a strong socialist-communist movement, a devastating economic crisis, and the still-fresh memory of a catastrophic war. Instead, the same conditions which might have brought revolution gave rise to that monstrous mutation, Nazism. Marxist scholars went into a dither of analysis to explain it.

I don't mean to pick on Marxists. But if they, probably the best equipped theoretically, the most committed and motivated to understand society, kept being bewildered, that suggests how impenetrable has been the mystery of social change in our time.

Who would have predicted the bizarre events of World War II—

the Nazi-Soviet pact (those embarrassing photos of von Ribbentrop and Molotov shaking hands), and the German army rolling through Russia, causing colossal casualties, apparently invincible, and then being turned back at the gates of Leningrad, on the edge of Moscow, in the streets of Stalingrad, and then surrounded, decimated, and defeated, the strutting Hitler at the end huddled in his bunker, waiting to die?

And then the post-war world, taking a shape no one could have drawn in advance. The Chinese Communist Revolution, which Stalin himself had given little chance. And then the turns of that revolution: the break with the Soviet Union, the tumultuous and violent Cultural Revolution, and then another turnabout, with post-Mao China renouncing its most fervently-held ideas and institutions, making overtures to the West, cuddling up to capitalist enterprise, perplexing everyone.

No one foresaw the disintegration of the old Western empires happening so quickly after the war, or the odd array of societies that would be created in the newly independent nations, from the benign socialism of Nyerere's Tanzania to the madness of Idi Amin's Uganda.

Spain became an astonishment. A million died in the civil war which ended in victory for the Fascist Franco. I recall a veteran of the Abraham Lincoln Brigade telling me that he could not imagine Fascism being overthrown in Spain without another bloody war. After Franco was gone, and a parliamentary democracy, open to Socialists, Communists, anarchists, everyone, was established in Spain, that same man expressed his awe that it all happened without the fratricide so many thought was inevitable.

In other places too, deeply-entrenched regimes seemed to suddenly disintegrate—in Portugal, Argentina, the Philippines, Iran.

The end of World War II left two superpowers with their respective spheres of influence and control, vying for military and political

power. The United States and the Soviet Union soon had 10,000 ther-
monuclear bombs each, enough to devastate the earth several times
over. The international scene was dominated by their rivalry, and it
was supposed that all affairs, in every nation, were affected by their
looming presence.

Yet, the most striking fact about these superpowers in 1988 is that,
despite their size, their wealth, their overwhelming accumulation of
nuclear weapons, they have been unable to control events, even in
those parts of the world considered to be their spheres of influence.

The Soviet Union, apparently successful in crushing revolts in
Hungary and Czechoslovakia, has had to accommodate itself to the
quick withdrawal of Yugoslavia from its orbit, the liberalization of
Hungary in recent years, and the continued power of the Solidarity
movement in Poland. Gorbachev's recent declarations about a new era
in Soviet relations with the Warsaw Pact nations is a recognition of the
inability of Soviet power to permanently suppress the desire for independence in neighboring countries.

The failure of the Soviet Union to have its way in Afghanistan,
its decision to withdraw after almost a decade of ugly intervention,
is the most striking evidence that even the possession of thermonu-
clear weapons does not guarantee domination over a determined
population.

The United States has more and more faced the same reality.

It could send an army into Korea but could not win, and was
forced to sign a compromise peace. It waged a full-scale war in
Indochina, the most brutal bombardment of a tiny peninsula in world
history, and yet was forced to withdraw. And in Latin America, after a
long history of U.S. military intervention, with Yankee imperialism
having its way again and again, this superpower, with all its wealth, all
its weapons, found itself frustrated. It was unable to prevent a revolution in Cuba, and after succeeding in organizing a counter-revolution

in Chile, could not prevent or overthrow a revolution in Nicaragua. For the first time, the nations of Latin America are refusing to do the bidding of *los norteamericanos*.

In the headlines every day, we see other instances of the failure of the presumably powerful over the presumably powerless: the inability of white South Africa to suppress the insurgency of the black majority; the inability of Israel, a nuclear power with formidable conventional arms, to contain the rebellion of Palestinians armed with stones in the West Bank and Gaza Strip.

This recitation of facts about twentieth century history, this evidence of unpredictability in human affairs, might be rather dull, except that it does lead us to some important conclusions.

The first is that the struggle for justice should never be abandoned because of the apparent overwhelming power of those who have the guns and the money and who seem invincible in their determination to hold on to it. That apparent power has, again and again, proved vulnerable to human qualities less measurable than bombs and dollars: moral fervor, determination, unity, organization, sacrifice, wit, ingenuity, courage, patience—whether by blacks in Alabama and South Africa, peasants in El Salvador, Nicaragua, and Vietnam, or workers and intellectuals in Poland, Hungary, and the Soviet Union itself. No cold calculation of the balance of power need deter people who are persuaded that their cause is just.

The second is that, in the face of the manifest unpredictability of social phenomena, all of history's excuses for war and preparation for war—self-defense, national security, freedom, justice, stopping aggression—can no longer be accepted. Nor can civil war be tolerated. Massive violence, whether in war or internal upheaval, cannot be justified by any end, however noble, *because no outcome is sure*. Indeed, the most certain characteristic of any upheaval, like war or revolution, is its uncertainty. Any humane and reasonable person must conclude that if the ends, however desirable, are uncertain, and the means are horrible and certain, those means must not be employed.

This is a persuasive argument, it seems to me, to direct at all those people, whether in the United States or elsewhere, who are still intoxicated by the analogy of World War II, who still distinguish between "just and unjust wars" (a universal belief shared by the Catholic Church, the capitalist West, and the Soviet Union), and who are willing to commit atrocities, whether on Hiroshima or in Budapest, for some good cause.

It is also an argument that needs to be examined seriously by those who, in this world of vicious nationalism, terrible poverty, and the waste of enormous resources on militarism and war, understand the need for radical change. Such change is needed, yet it must be accomplished without massive violence. This is the great challenge to human ingenuity in our time. It is a challenge to blacks in South Africa, to Palestinians in the Occupied Territories (both of whom seem to understand it), as well as to Americans and Russians disgusted with their governments' robbery of national resources for profit and power.

The recognition of unpredictability is troubling. But all we have lost are our illusions about power and about violence. What we gain is an understanding that the means we use to struggle for justice, even for revolutionary change, must scrupulously observe human rights. The lives and liberties of ordinary people must not be sacrificed, either by government or by revolutionaries, certain that they know the end results of what they do, indifferent to their own ignorance.

4

Failure to Quit

This essay, written for *Z Magazine* in 1990, and reprinted in my book *Failure to Quit*, was inspired (if you are willing to call this an inspired piece) by my students of the Eighties. I was teaching a spring and fall lecture course with four hundred students in each course (and yet with lots of discussion). I looked hard, listened closely, but did not find the apathy, the conservatism, the disregard for the plight of others, that everybody (right and left) was reporting about "the me generation."

I can understand pessimism, but I don't believe in it. It's not simply a matter of faith, but of historical evidence. Not overwhelming evidence, just enough to give hope, because for hope we don't need certainty, only possibility. Which (despite all those confident statements that "history shows..."and "history proves...") is all history can offer us.

When I hear so often that there is little hope for change from the present generation of young people, I think back to the despair that accompanied the onset of the Sixties.

Historians of the late Forties and Fifties (Richard Hofstadter, Louis

Hartz) were writing ruefully about a liberal-conservative "consensus" that dominated the United States all through its history and that still prevailed, setting severe limits to change. Herbert Marcuse, at the start of the Sixties, saw American society, American thought, as "one-dimensional," with radical ideas absorbed and deflected, dissent repressed through "tolerance."

One could not read these men, socially conscious, desirous themselves of change yet despairing of it, without feeling a deep pessimism about the possibilities for change in the United States. As the year 1960 began, Princeton philosopher Walter Kaufmann lamented "the uncommitted generation" and wrote: "What distinguishes them is that they are not committed to any cause." Neither he nor Hofstadter, Hartz, Marcuse, nor anyone for that matter, could have predicted what would soon happen.

It was on the first of February in that first year of the new decade that four black students from North Carolina A & T College sat down at a "white" lunch counter in Greensboro, refused to move, and were arrested. In two weeks, sit-ins had spread to fifteen cities in five Southern states. By the year's end, 50,000 people had participated in demonstrations in a hundred cities, and 3,600 had been put in jail.

That was the start of the civil rights movement, which became an anti-war movement, a women's movement, a cultural upheaval, and in its course hundreds of thousands, no, millions of people became committed for a short time, or for a lifetime. It was unprecedented, unpredicted, and for at least fifteen years, uncontrollable. It would shake the country and startle the world, with consequences we are hardly aware of today.

True, those consequences did not include the end of war, exploitation, hunger, racism, military intervention, nationalism, sexism—only the end of legal racial segregation, the end of the war of Vietnam, the end of illegal abortions. It was just a beginning.

The uncommitted generation? I thought so too when, out of the Air Force, married, with two small children, finishing graduate work in history at Columbia University, I went South to teach in Atlanta, Georgia. My job was at Spelman College, where young black women, the daughters of railroad porters, teachers, ministers, maids, laborers, farmers, came to get their degrees. It was 1956. The atmosphere on that tree-lined, fragrant campus was sedate, quiet, careful, and only close attention to what was said and left unsaid revealed deep resentment just below the surface. By 1960, these same quiet students were sitting-in, demonstrating, picketing, going to jail. I learned that it was a serious mistake to interpret lack of action as lack of thought, lack of feeling. Rather, it was the absence of opportunities, openings, examples to emulate, groups to join—but when those appeared, the silence changed to uproar.

There is no such uproar today. There is an uncertain mixture of silence and commotion. The silence deserves attention. In 1984 there was a silent majority in this country that refused to vote for Reagan: 68 percent of the eligible voters (add the 21 percent who voted for Mondale with the 47 percent who didn't bother to vote). This leaves 32 percent who voted for Reagan, which was converted by a timid press and a gullible public into an "overwhelming mandate."

But there is more than silence.

There is a human carry-over from the Sixties. True, there are veterans of those movements who have been swallowed up by the gluttonous tigers of survival and "success" and live, happily or not, inside the bellies of those beasts, making do. But there are others, in the cages, yes, but holding off the carnivores with a chair and a prayer, stubbornly refusing to be eaten, looking for openings and opportunities, pushing the system to its limits while pointing beyond, keeping the spirit of resistance alive.

I think of two of my students at Spelman, among the many who were jailed during the Atlanta sit-ins: Marian Wright, going to Yale Law School, and to Mississippi with the Movement, now the tireless head of the Children's Defense Fund in Washington; Alice Walker, becoming a poet, a novelist, a feminist and political activist. I think of Carolyn Mugar, working with anti-war GIs in the Vietnam years, more recently a labor organizer in southern Massachusetts. Or Bernice Reagon, student leader and Freedom Singer in the Albany, Georgia Movement of 1961-62, now a folk historian at the Smithsonian, a formidable mind and voice, still a Freedom Singer ("Sweet Honey in the Rock"). And Staughton Lynd, historian, organizer of Freedom Schools in Mississippi, anti-war protester of the Sixties, now a labor lawyer in Ohio.

We all know such people, but it goes far beyond personal connections. There are thousands of local groups around the country—many more than existed in the Sixties—devoted to struggling for tenants' rights or women's rights, or environmental protection, or against the arms race, or to take care of the hungry and the homeless, or those in need of health care. There are now tens of thousands of professionals, many of them veterans of the movements of the Sixties, who bring unorthodox ideas and humane values into courtrooms, classrooms, hospitals.

Over 50,000 people have signed the Pledge of Resistance, committing themselves to protest against U.S. intervention in Central America. A small number, but it represents a large part of the nation, because survey after survey shows a majority of the country opposed to administration policy in Central America. Is it not reasonable to assume that a U.S. invasion of Nicaragua, so lusted after by the Reagan Administration, was forestalled, despite a timid Congress, by recognition that the public would not support such an action?

When activists commit civil disobedience to protest against the CIA or the arms race, or aid to the contras, the degree of their distance from the general sentiment can be measured, at least roughly, by how juries of ordinary citizens react. During the war in Vietnam, when religious pacifists entered draft boards illegally to destroy draft records as a way of protesting the war, juries became increasingly reluctant to convict, and near the end of the war we saw the dramatic acquittal of the Camden 28 by a jury which then threw a party for the defendants.

Acts of civil disobedience today, at a much earlier stage of U.S. intervention, are getting verdicts of acquittal when juries are permitted to listen to the defendants' reasons for their civil disobedience. In the spring of 1984, in Burlington, Vermont, the "Winooski 44" had occupied Senator Stafford's office to protest his support of aid to the contras. The jury heard many hours of testimony about conditions in Nicaragua, the role of the CIA, the nature of the contras, and voted for acquittal. One of the jurors, a local house painter, said: "I was honored to be on that jury. I felt a part of history."

In Minneapolis that same year, seven "trespassers" protesting at the Honeywell Corporation were acquitted. In 1985, men and women blocked the Great Lakes Training Station in Illinois, others blocked the South African Embassy in Chicago, nineteen people in the state of Washington halted trains carrying warheads, and all these won acquittals in court. Last year in western Massachusetts, where a protest against the CIA took place, there was another surprising acquittal. One of the jurors, Donna L. Moody, told a reporter: "All the expert testimony against the CIA was alarming. It was very educational."

Over the past six years, eighteen "Plowshares" actions, involving symbolic sabotage of nuclear weaponry, have resulted mostly in guilty verdicts. In the latest case, involving two Catholic priests and two others who broke into a naval air station near Philadelphia and damaged three aircraft, the judge refused the defense of "necessity" but allowed the jury to hear the defendants' reasons for their actions. The jury was unable to reach a verdict.

Several years ago, when Reagan announced the blockade of Nicaragua, 550 of us sat-in at the federal building in Boston to protest, and were arrested. It seemed too big a group of dissidents to deal with, and charges were dropped. When I received my letter, I saw for the first time what the official complaint against all of us was: "Failure to Quit." That is, surely, the critical fact about the continuing movement for human rights here and all over the world.

We hear many glib dismissals of today's college students as being totally preoccupied with money and self. In fact, there is much concern among students with their economic futures—evidence of the failure of the economic system to provide for the young, more than a sign of their indifference to social injustice. But the past few years have seen political actions on campuses all over the country. For 1986 alone, a partial list shows: 182 students, calling for divestment from South Africa, arrested at the University of Texas; a black-tie dinner for alumni at Harvard called off after a protest on South African holdings; charges dropped against 49 Wellesley protesters after half the campus boycotted classes in support; and more protests recorded at Yale, Wisconsin, Louisville, San Jose, Columbia.

But what about the others, the non-protesting students? Among the liberal arts students, business majors, and ROTC cadets who sit in my classes, there are super-patriots and enthusiasts of capitalism, but also others, whose thoughts deserve some attention:

Writing in his class journal, one ROTC student, whose father was a navy flier, his brother a navy commander:

This one class made me go out and read up on South Africa. What I learned made me sick. My entire semester has been a paradox. I go to your class and I see a Vietnam vet named Joe Bangert tell of his experiences in the war. I was enthralled by his talk...By the end of that hour and a half I hated the Vietnam war as much as he did. The only problem is that three hours after that class I am marching around in my uniform...and feeling great about it. Is there something wrong with me? Am I being hypocritical? Sometimes I don't know...

Young woman in ROTC: "What really stuck in my mind was the ignorance some people displayed at the end of class. We were discussing welfare. Some students stated that people on welfare were lazy, that if they really wanted to, they could find jobs. Argg! These rich kids (or middle class or whatever) who have all they need and think they're so superior make me angry..."

The same student, after seeing the film *Hearts and Minds*:

General Westmoreland said "Orientals don't value lives." I was incredulous. And then they showed the little boy holding the picture of his father and he was crying and crying and crying...I must admit I started crying. What's worse was that I was wearing my Army uniform that day and I had to make a conscious effort not to disappear in my seat.

Young woman in the School of Management:

North broke the law, but will he be punished?... If he is let off the hook then all of America is punished. Every inner-city kid who is sent to jail for stealing food to feed his brothers and sisters is punished. Every elderly person who has to fight just to keep warm on a winter night will be punished.... The law is supposed to be the common bond—the peace making body. Yet it only serves the function selectively—just when the people in control wish it to.

Surely history does not start anew with each decade. The roots of one era branch and flower in subsequent eras. Human beings, writings, invisible transmitters of all kinds, carry messages across the generations. I try to be pessimistic, to keep up with some of my friends. But I think back over the decades, and look around. And then, it seems to me that the future is not certain, but it is possible.

5

The Spirit of
Rebellion

Writing a column to appear in the July 4, 1975 issue of the *Boston Globe,* I wanted to break away from the traditional celebrations of Independence Day, in which the spirit of that document, with its call for rebellion and revolution, was most often missing. The column appeared with the title "The Brooklyn Bridge and the Spirit of the Fourth."

In New York, a small army of policemen, laid off and angry, have been blocking the Brooklyn Bridge, and garbage workers are letting the refuse pile up in the streets. In Boston, some young people on Mission Hill are illegally occupying an abandoned house to protest the demolition of a neighborhood. And elderly people, on the edge of survival, are fighting Boston Edison's attempt to raise the price of electricity.

So it looks like a good Fourth of July, with a spirit of rebellion proper to the Declaration of Independence.

The Declaration, adopted 199 years ago today, says (although those in high office don't like to be reminded) that government is not sacred, that it is set up to give people an equal right to life, liberty, and the pursuit of happiness and that if it fails to do this, we have a right to "alter or abolish it."

The Declaration of Independence became an embarrassment to the Founding Fathers almost immediately. Some of George Washington's soldiers resented the rich in New York, Boston, and Philadelphia, profiting from the war. When the Continental Congress in 1781 voted half pay for life to officers of the Revolution and nothing for enlisted men, there was mutiny in the New Jersey and Pennsylvania lines. Washington ordered two young mutineers shot "as an example." The shovelfuls of earth covering their bodies also smudged the words of the Declaration, five years old and already ignored, that "all men are created equal."

Black slaves in Boston took those words seriously, too, and, during the Revolution, petitioned the Massachusetts General Court for their freedom. But the Revolution was not fought for them.

It did not seem to be fought for the poor white farmers either, who, after serving in the war, now faced high taxes, and seizure of homes and livestock for nonpayment. In western Massachusetts, they organized, blocking the doors of courthouses to prevent foreclosures. This was Shay's Rebellion. The militia finally routed them, and the Founding Fathers hurried to Philadelphia to write the Constitution, to set up a government where such rebellions could be controlled.

Arguing for the Constitution, James Madison said it would hold back "a rage for paper money, for an abolition of debts, for an equal division of property, or for any other improper or wicked project..." The Constitution took the stirring phrase of the Declaration, "life, liberty and the pursuit of happiness" and changed it to "life, liberty and property." The Declaration was only a historic document. The Constitution became the law of the land.

Both documents were written by whites. Many of these were slaveholders. All were men. Women gathered in 1848 in Seneca Falls, New York, and adopted their own Declaration: "We hold these truths to be self-evident: that all men and women are created equal..."

The Constitution was written by the rich, who set up a government to protect their property. Gerald Ford is still doing it. They say he is a "good guy." He certainly has been good to big business. He has arranged for gasoline prices and heating bills to go up while the oil companies make enormous profits. He vetoed a bill to allow an interest rate for homeowners of 6 percent while the nation's ten biggest banks made $2 billion in profits last year.

Unemployment, food and rent are all rising; but $7 billion in tax breaks went to 160,000 very wealthy people last year, according to a congressional report.

No wonder the spirit of rebellion is growing. No wonder that even police, paid to be keepers of law and order and laid-off when they have served their purpose, are catching a bit of that spirit.

It is fitting for this Fourth of July, this anniversary of the Declaration of Independence.

6

Non-Violent
Direct Action

The experience of the civil rights movement forced me to think about the process of social change—about the alternatives of violence and parliamentary reform, and about the principle that was at the heart of the Southern movement for equal rights—non-violent direct action. I presented this paper at the 1965 annual meeting of the American Orthopsychiatric Association in New York, and it was published in the *American Journal of Orthopsychiatry,* January, 1966.

In 1937 sociologist Robert S. Lynd wrote a little gem of a book entitled *Knowledge for What?* in which he attacked the divorce of scholarship from the problems of his day. The book has just been reissued 27 years later. In the interim the world has experienced Auschwitz and Hiroshima and Birmingham, yet the accusation in that book against the world of scholarship remains exactly as true in every line. Social scientists for the most part still are not focusing their research directly on the world's urgent problems. True, they are accumulating data on these problems, but too often they avoid moving too close to the presentation of solutions because at that point controversy enters. So the scholarly monographs and the social evils keep rising higher and higher in separate piles, parallel to one another with such Euclidian perfection that we begin to despair they ever will intersect.

I would like in this brief paper to at least initiate a discussion on the uses of power, not as an academic exercise, but in relation to what we see around us and to what we hear, which is more and more these days the sound of crowds in the streets.

The health of society, I assume, is dependent on a balance between people's expectations and the fulfillment of those expectations. Both the Buddhism of Gautama in the East and the Stoicism of Epictetus in the West in their emphasis on resignation as a means to happiness were fitted to the limits of a crude technology. Today the momentum of science has created worldwide waves of demand which *can* be fulfilled. Quiescence and resignation are no longer pertinent, and the clamor everywhere for change, though expressed in passion, is reasonable.

There is little question any more that change in our social institutions must come. Never before in history has there been such a consensus in objectives all over the world, nor such a variance of method in trying to achieve these objectives. Most men everywhere agree they want to end war, imperialism, racism, poverty, disease and tyranny. What they disagree about is whether these expectations can be fulfilled within the old frameworks of nationalism, representative government and the profit system. And running through the tension between agreement and disagreement are these questions: How much violence will be necessary to fulfill these expectations? What must we suffer to get the world we all want?

We have three traditional ways of satisfying the need for institutional change: war, revolution, and gradual reform. We might define war as violence from without, revolution as violence from within and gradual reform as deferred violence. I would like to examine all three in the new light of the mid-twentieth century.

Assuming that change always involves a degree of dislocation and of social cost, man's problem is then how to achieve maximum desirable change at minimum cost. War at best has been a haphazard way of deciding this question, for the impetus of war piles up the dead with little regard for social consequence, so that even those wars fought against the most obvious of evils, such as the Civil War (with Negro slavery at stake) and World War II (with global slavery at stake), brought in the first case the uncontrolled gushing of what Edmund Wilson calls "patriotic gore" and in the second the needless bombings of Dresden and Hiroshima. At its worst, war has been mass slaughter without even the saving grace of a definable social goal. The Trojan War was the first and classic case, and that element of idiocy has persisted in all wars in varying degree.

Up to the hydrogen bomb, it was still possible to weigh cost and consequence. Now we can throw away the scales, for it should be clear to any rational and humane person that there is no piece of territory (not Berlin or Viet Nam or Hungary), there is no social system yet put into operation anywhere by man (not socialism or capitalism or whatever) which is worth the consequence of atomic war. If war ever in its shotgun way represented a method of achieving social progress, the illimitable scale of warfare today removes it forever as a justifiable method of social change. John U. Nef of the University of Chicago put it this way in his book *War and Human Progress*, which he wrote soon after World War II:

> The only justification for war is the defense of a culture worth defending, and the states of the modern world have less and less to defend beyond their material comforts, in spite of the claims of some to represent fresh concepts of civilization. The new weapons have made nonsense of defen-

sive war. Peoples have been left without any means of defending except by destroying others, and the destruction is almost certain to be mutual.

What of revolution? Here the balance of achievement and cost is less haphazard, though still far from rational. The four great revolutions of modern times (the American, the French, the Russian and the Chinese) though all erratic in their movement towards social progress, in the end, I believe, justified the relatively small amount of violence required to fulfill them. But today, can we still look to revolutions as the chief means of social change, and as a useful means, whereby great change can be achieved at relatively small cost?

In some exceptional instances, yes. But, as a general rule, it seems to me that the conditions of the contemporary world have removed the feasibility of revolutions in the old sense. There are several reasons for this. One is that the power of weapons in the hands of the ruling elite makes popular uprisings, however great is the base of support, a very dubious undertaking. The other consideration, and probably more important, is that revolutions like wars no longer can be contained. They almost always involve one or more of the great nations of the world, and are either crushed by an outside power (as were the Hungarians in their revolt) or are prolonged to the point of frightful massacre (as the revolt in Viet Nam was met by the intervention of the French and then the Americans, and as the revolt in the Congo was stymied by Belgians and other forces). The Cuban revolution was an oddity; it was able to subsist because it brought into the picture not one but both the two leading world powers. There, even in success we can see the perils posed by revolution in the contemporary world, for the Cuban missile crisis almost set off a global disaster.

This removal of both war and revolution as methods of ushering in the inevitable changes would seem to leave us with the stock-in-trade of Western liberals: gradual reform. Here the United States is the prime example of peaceful accommodation, harmonizing gracefully with the requirements of change.

There is a double trouble with this pleasant solution: it does not square with the facts of the American past, and it does not fit the requirements of the American future. Let me explain what I mean.

It is remarkable how many persons, both in the United States and abroad, accept the legend that our country is the quintessential example of peaceful, progressive development as opposed to the violent change characteristic of other parts of the world. Yet the United States was born in violent revolution, and then solved its chief domestic problem not by reform but by one of the bloodiest wars in modern times. Its history has been punctuated with bursts of violence. Each outbreak was a reminder, quickly forgotten, that the changes we made through gradual reform were not fast enough or large enough to match the growing expectations of sections of the population: the slow steps made against slavery, for instance (the abolition of the slave trade as agreed to in Philadelphia in 1787, the Compromise of 1820 and the Compromise of 1850) were all failures, and the Civil War resulted.

Congress did not move fast enough to alleviate the pains of exploitation for the new industrial working class of the latter half of the nineteenth century, and so the period from 1877 to 1914 saw a series of labor explosions unmatched in their ferocity in any country in the world: the railroad insurrections of 1877, the Haymarket killings of 1886, the Homestead strike of 1894, the textile strike at Lawrence in 1912 and the Ludlow Massacre in Colorado in 1914. What, if not the failure of American reformism, explains the growth of the Socialist Party to a million supporters in 1912, the emergence of the Industrial Workers of the World as a radical, militant labor union devoted to the abolition of the capitalist system? It took the hysteria of world war to help crush both these movements.

How successful was the reform of the Progressive Era of Theodore Roosevelt and Woodrow Wilson when the whole structure they built up to keep the economy intact (Federal Reserve System, Federal Trade Commission, antitrust legislation) collapsed in 1929, and ushered in another decade of violence (bonus marches and marches of the unemployed, of sit-down strikes and clashes between workingmen and police) and again ended not in prosperity but in war? Is it New Deal reform or war expenditures that keep today's economy from collapsing into another period of violent conflict? Can we really say that the history of our nation is of carefully phased reform measures, of peaceful evolution towards domestic prosperity and national peace?

And now, in this last decade, we suddenly have learned that what we thought was gradual progress towards ending race prejudice in the United States was not nearly sufficient. It has taken mass demonstrations in Montgomery, Alabama; mass arrests in Albany, Georgia; the violence of the Freedom Rides; the bombings in Birmingham, and the murders in Mississippi to make us aware of the failure of piecemeal reform to establish racial justice in America.

There are lessons in this, I believe, far beyond the race crisis in the United States, and I want to explore some of them. My point is that gradualism, even in that presumed mecca of reform, the U.S.A., never really has matched the push of events, and that today the momentum of world change has made it even less able to do so. Thus, *none* of the traditionally approved mechanisms for social change (not war, nor revolution, nor reform) is adequate for the kind of problems we face today in the United States and in the world. We need apparently some technique which is more energetic than parliamentary reform and yet not subject to the dangers which war and revolution pose in the atomic age.

This technique, I suggest, is that which has been used over the centuries by aggrieved groups in fitful, semi-conscious control of their own actions. With the Negro revolt in America, the technique has begun to take on the quality of a deliberate use of power to effect the most change with the least harm. I speak of non-violent direct action. This encompasses a great variety of methods, limited only by our imaginations: sit-ins, freedom rides and freedom walks, prayer pilgrimages, wade-ins, pray-ins, freedom ballots, freedom schools, and who knows what is on the horizon? Whatever the specific form, this technique has certain qualities: it disturbs the status quo, it intrudes on the complacency of the majority, it expresses the anger and the hurt of the aggrieved, it publicizes an injustice, it demonstrates the inadequacy of whatever reforms have been instituted up to that point, it creates tension and trouble and thus forces the holders of power to move faster than they otherwise would have to redress grievances.

The crucial problems of our time no longer can be left to simmer on the low flame of gradualism, only to explode. Poverty, for instance, will not be attacked on the scale which is required until the ease of the well off is punctured in some brusque way. And in this shrinking world, for how long can the United Sates contain its vast wealth inside the national membrane and spend billions on useless products while a million people starve in Calcutta? Once people begin to measure the distribution of wealth on global lines there may well be a clamor against the deformed concentration of it in one country of the world. Jet travel makes the world smaller than the Roman Empire. Then why shouldn't the parallel existence of America and India be as much as object of concern as the parallel existence in Rome of the opulence of emperors and the misery of slaves? And how else will horror be expressed under conditions of today except by some form of popular protest?

Consider another issue: with the possession of nuclear bombs proliferating in the world and with the mathematical probability of war by error increasing, can we depend on the normal parliamentary processes for concerned people to express to the powers of the world their revulsion against war? Should we not have an increasing number of those little bands of pacifists, from Bertrand Russell to the ones who sailed into the Pacific on the *Golden Rule?*

Also there is the problem of freedom for dissenters, which exists in East and West, North and South, in communist and capitalist countries, in the old nations and in the new nations. How else but by Poznan uprisings, by demonstrations and civil disobedience, can such freedom be maintained and extended?

For us in the United States, it is hard to accept the idea that the ordinary workings of the parliamentary system will not suffice in the world today. But recall that Jefferson himself, watching the Constitution being created, and thinking of Shay's Rebellion, spoke of the need for revolutions every twenty years. And Rousseau, at the very moment representative government was beginning to take hold, pointed to the inability of anyone to truly represent anyone else's interests. And Robert Michels, the Swiss sociologist, 150 years after Rousseau, showed us how an "iron law of oligarchy" operates within any government or any party to separate top from bottom and to make power-holders insensitive to the needs of the mass. No matter how democratic elections are, they represent only fleeting and widely separated moments of popular participation. In that long span between elections, people are passive and captive.

Thus, we face a dilemma: wars and revolutions today cannot be limited and are therefore very perilous. Yet parliamentary reform is inadequate. We need some intermediate device, powerful but restrained and explosive but controlled, to pressure and even to shock the decision-makers into making the kinds of changes in institutions which fit our world. Walter Millis, in an essay written for the Center for the Study of Democratic Institutions, has argued persuasively that the price we may have to pay for a world without war is a kind of intermittent guerrilla warfare, constantly bringing society into rough accord with popular demands. It turns out (and we have the experience of all bourgeois, socialist and national revolutions to support this) that *no* form of government, once in power, can be trusted to limit its own ambition, to extend freedom and to wither away. This means that it is up to the citizenry, those outside of power, to engage in permanent combat with the state, short of violent, escalatory revolution, but beyond the gentility of the ballot-box, to insure justice, freedom and well being, all those values which virtually the entire world has come to believe in.

This idea links the Negro uprising in America to the turmoil everywhere in the world. It also links present to past, for what I am suggesting is a more deliberate, more conscious, more organized use of those techniques of constructive dissent which man has used in spontaneity and in desperation throughout history.

Those of us reared in the tradition of liberal, gradualist reform, and cherishing tranquillity, may have to learn to sacrifice a little of these in order not to lose all of them. Such a course may not be easy, but it is not a bad substitute for the world as we have known it up to now, a world of simplistic and terrible solutions, where we oscillated constantly between two alternatives: the devastation of war or the injustice of peace.

PART 2

On Electoral Politics

7

The Great Silence

As the presidential race for the year 2000 got under way, it became clear that all the candidates, Democrat and Republican, were ignoring those aspects of of American policy which had the most consequences for the people of the world—war, militarism, and what the World Bank called a "silent genocide," the deaths by malnutrition and sickness of millions of children.

Every day, as the soggy rhetoric of the presidential candidates accumulates into an enormous pile of solid waste, we get more and more evidence of the failure of the American political system. The candidates for the job of leader of the most powerful country in the world have nothing important to say. On domestic issues, they offer platitudes about health care and social security and taxes which are meaningless given the record of both political parties. And on foreign policy, utter silence.

That silence is what I want to talk about.

In domestic policy, there are enough slight differences among the candidates to make some liberals and progressives, desperate for hopeful signs, seize upon the most feeble of promises. No candidate, Democrat or Republican, as they propose lame and wobbly steps towards taking care of some fraction of the forty million uninsured, suggests universal, non-profit, government-guaranteed health care. None of them, muttering unintelligibly about one or another tax plan, talk about taxing the wealth and income of the super-rich in such a way as to make several trillion dollars available for housing, health, jobs, education.

But in foreign and military policy, there are not even mutterings about change. All the candidates vie with one another in presenting themselves as supporters of the military, desirous of building our military strength. Here is Mr. Universe, bulging ridiculously with muscles useless for nothing except winning contests and bullying the other kids on the block (it is important to be #1, important to maintain "credibility"), promising to buy more body-building equipment, and asking all of us to pay for it.

How can we, if we have any self-respect, support candidates—Republican or Democrat—who have nothing to say about the fact that the United States, with 4% of the world's population, consumes 25% of its wealth, who have nothing to say about our obligation to the other 96%, many of whom are suffering as a result of American policy?

What is that obligation? First, to follow the principle of the physicians' Hippocratic Oath, "Do No Harm." Instead, we are doing much harm. By depriving the people of Iraq of food, medicine, and vital equipment, we are causing them enormous suffering, under the pretense of "sending a message" to Saddam Hussein. It appears we have no other way to send a message but through killing people. How does this differ, except in scale, from the killings done by terrorists around the world, who also defend their acts by their need to "send a message."

Similarly with the Cuban embargo. We pretend we care about "democracy" in Cuba, we who have supported dictatorship there and all over Latin America for a hundred years. Truth is, we cannot bear the thought that Castro for forty years has defied us, refused the homage—its material form being part of the world capitalist club—to which we are accustomed in this hemisphere. And there are precious votes in Florida, more precious than any possible deprivation for the children of Cuba.

Which candidate, Democrat or Republican, has had the decency to speak out on this? What meaning has the phrase "human rights" if people are denied the necessities of life?

Which of them has said a word about our obscene possession of thousands of nuclear weapons—while Washington goes into hysterics over the possibility that some country in the Middle East may some day have one nuclear bomb? None of them has the courage to say what common sense tells us, and what someone so expert on military issues and so tied to the Establishment as Paul Nitze (an ambassador-at-large in the Reagan administration) has publicly said: "I see no compelling reason why we should not unilaterally get rid of our nuclear weapons....It is the presence of nuclear weapons that threatens our existence."

While the front pages report the latest solemn pronouncements of the candidates, claiming to care about the well-being of Americans, the inside pages report the brutal Russian assault on Chechnya, with not a word from these candidates about the well-being of men, women, and children huddled in the basements of Grozny, awaiting the next wave of bombings.

There have been a few lame expressions of protest from the Clinton administration, but it is careful not to offend the Russian leaders, and so last October, *The Toronto Sun* reported: "In Moscow, standing next to her beaming Russian hosts, U.S. Secretary of State

Madeleine Albright proclaimed 'we are opposed to terrorism,' meaning Islamic rebels in the Caucasus fighting Russian rule." We can't forget that Clinton supported the Russian war on Chechnya from 1994 to 1996, going so far (he does get carried away) as to compare Chechnya to the Confederacy of the Civil War, which had to be put down for the sake of the larger nation. Yeltsin as Lincoln—that does seem a bit of a stretch.

Is it possible that the various candidates, all supported by huge corporate wealth (it is expected that three billion dollars will be spent for the elections of the year 2000), do not dare challenge a foreign policy whose chief motivation is not human rights but business profit? Behind the coldness to the people of Chechnya—there is the crass matter of oil in that part of the world.

Last November, Stephen Kinzer of *The New York Times* reported from Istanbul:

> "Four nations in the Caspian Sea region took a giant step today toward embracing one of President Clinton's cherished foreign policy projects, a pipeline that would assure Western control over the potentially vast oil and natural gas reserves...and give the United States greater influence in the region."

The word "cherished" suggests an emotional attachment one cannot find with regard to human rights in the Third World.

Does Clinton equally "cherish" projects designed to eliminate hunger and illness in the world?

The World Health Organization has described the plight of ten million people in the world—dying of AIDS or tuberculosis—as "a silent genocide."

The numbers make it as serious and frightening as Hitler's genocide, which our political leaders regularly deplore, at no cost to them. But no candidate proposes that we stop spending several hundred billions on the military, stop selling arms to countries all over the world, stop the use of land mines, stop training the officers of military dictatorships in the Third World—and use that money to wipe out tuberculosis and try to stem the spread of AIDS.

The candidate Gore, speaking to the UN Security Council a few weeks ago, and required to say something about the epidemic, promised to increase the U.S. commitment to fight AIDS up to $325 million. That is a tinier commitment than that of other industrialized countries, and less than the money spent for one fighter-bomber. That sum should be compared to $1.6 billion dollars proposed by the Clinton administration for Colombia to deal with drugs, but perhaps really to deal with rebellion.

I suppose the problem is that people who are being bombed around the world, or people who are dying as the result of preventable illnesses, do not vote in American elections. If our political system is not sensitive to human suffering in this country where there are no votes to be counted—the homeless, the imprisoned, the very poor—how can we expect it to care a whit about people a thousand miles from our voting booths, however miserable their situation?

Since our political system—bi-partisan in its coldness to human rights—determines that no candidate will talk about this, such a system cannot be respected. It can only be protested against, challenged, or, in the words of the Declaration of Independence, referring to a government that has violated its responsibility to its people, "altered or abolished." That's a tall order, but it can be prepared for by a multitude of short steps, in which citizens act, outside of the party system, to redress their grievances. Ultimately, the power of government, of big business, is fragile. We have seen this many times in history. When people, moved by indignation, wanting to live in a decent society, act together, a new and irresistible power is created, and democracy comes alive.

8

On Presidential Liars

The year of 1998 was dominated in the news media by the sexual shenanigans of President Bill Clinton and a formerly obscure White House intern, Monica Lewinsky. This preoccupation illustrated perfectly the proclivity of the American media to fasten on the trivial at the expense of life-and death matters.

In all the excitement about Bill Clinton's sex life, and its repercussions on his presidency, have we as a nation lost—or did we never have—a sense of proportion?

Clinton has lied to us, deceived us, and then covered up his deceptions, about his sexual shenanigans—which, however odious, caused no one to lose a life. Many other presidents have lied to us, and deceived us, especially since World War II, about activities that we had every right to know about, in which thousands, even millions of people, lost their lives. Let's recall some of that history.

Let's start with Harry Truman, who lied to us and the world when he said the bomb dropped on Hiroshima was dropped on "a military target." Several hundred thousand civilians—men, women, children died. Truman also lied to the nation about our war in Korea, presenting this as necessary to stop the spread of Communism in the world (it did not, and indeed could not), to show that "aggression does not pay" (the world did not listen; aggressions continued), saying we were fighting for democracy (hardly, since South Korea was a military dictatorship). Over 50,000 Americans died. And perhaps two million Koreans.

Eisenhower lied about our spy flights over the Soviet Union, even after one flier on such a mission was shot down. He deceived the nation and the world about the United States involvement in the coup that overthrew a democratic government in Guatemala and put in place a military junta that then took thousands of lives. He deceived the nation about the U.S. role in subverting a government in Iran which offended the oil corporations. The Shah of Iran was put back on the throne, meaning death and torture for his opponents. (In many of these events, the actual deceptions were carried on by his underlings, but the fact is that Eisenhower knew of them, and approved of them.)

Kennedy lied to the nation about the U.S. involvement in the 1961 failed invasion of Cuba, telling a press conference: "I can assure you that the United States has no intention of using force to overthrow the Castro regime."

Kennedy, Johnson, and Nixon all lied to the nation about what was happening in Vietnam. Kennedy, while denying repeatedly that American fliers were involved in bombing of Vietnam, sent two helicopter companies there as early as 1962, and napalm began to be used. Johnson and Nixon both lied when they claimed only military targets were bombed (reporters knew the greatest number of deaths was among civilians). And Nixon deceived the nation about the secret bombing of Cambodia.

Reagan lied to the nation about his secret and illegal support of the contras in Nicaragua. He lied about the importance of Grenada in order to justify the American invasion of that little island. George Bush lied about the reasons for invading Panama, saying it was to stop the drug trade, but in fact the drug trade has flourished. And he deceived the nation about his real interest in the Persian Gulf, pretending to deep anguish about the fate of Kuwait, but actually more concerned about enhancing American power in Saudi Arabia and controlling the oil deposits of the region.

Against this history of lies that brought death to so many people, Clinton's deceptions are ludicrous. Politicians and journalists who are indignant that he lied about sex with "that woman," were silent when he deceived the nation about the need to bomb a "nerve gas plant" in the Sudan. His administration could produce no evidence that the plant was anything but what the Sudanese government said it was—a plant that produced medicines for the Sudanese people.

The president has lost his "moral authority," it is said, because of his lies about his sexual behavior. Did he—and indeed both Republicans and Democrats in Congress—not lose their moral authority when they took away basic benefits from single mothers, and food stamps from immigrants, when they failed to provide universal medical care, while spending hundreds of billions on an unnecessary military machine?

We are seeing a shocking loss of perspective on the part of political leaders, the press, and the public. If politicians and journalists have lost their sense of moral proportion, must we, as citizens lose ours? Should we not pull back from our obsession with lies about sex, and concentrate on finding out the truth about policies that mean life or death for people in this country and all over the world?

9

A Little Disquisition on Big Government

The Declaration of Independence, which is the quintessential document of democracy, discusses the origin and purpose of government. It says that we are all endowed "with certain unalienable rights, that among these are life, liberty, and the pursuit of happiness." It further says that "to secure these rights, governments are instituted among men, deriving their just powers from the consent of the governed." Well, if governments have the responsibility to secure for all of us our rights to life, liberty, and the pursuit of happiness, that is a big order, calling, it may well be argued, for "big government." This essay discusses the hypocrisy surrounding the cries of politicians—Democrats as well as Republicans—to do away with "big government."

I have seen some of my most stalwart friends flinch before the accusation that they—in asking, let us say, for a single-payer health care system—were calling for "big government." So insistent has been the press and the political leadership of the country—in both parties—that "big government" is a plague to be avoided, that otherwise courageous people on the Left have retreated before the attack.

It's an issue, therefore, that deserves some examination, using a bit of history.

When Clinton, in his 1996 campaign, announced happily that "the era of big government is over," he was suggesting that the United States had gone through an unfortunate phase which was now ended.

He was repeating the myth that there once was a golden past where the "free market" reigned and the nation followed Jefferson's dictum: "that government is best which governs least." Big government has been with the world for at least five hundred years, and became very big in this country (Jefferson never followed his own pronouncement, as he doubled the territory of the government with the Louisiana Purchase).

It was the rise of the modern national state in the 16th century that introduced big government, to centralize the tax system and thus raise enough money to subsidize the new world-wide trading organizations, like the Dutch East India Company and the British East India Company. Both of these companies were granted government charters around 1600, giving them monopoly rights to maraud around the world, trading goods and human beings, bringing wealth back to the home country.

The new national states now had to raise armies and navies, to protect the shipping trade (especially the slave trade) of these powerful companies, to invade other parts of the world, to forcibly take land, for trading and settling, from indigenous people. The state would use its power to drive out foreign competitors, to put down rebellions at home and abroad. "Big government" was needed, for the benefit of the mercantile and land-owning classes.

Adam Smith, considered the apostle of the "free market," understood very well how capitalism could not survive a truly free market, if government was not big enough to protect it. He wrote, in the middle of the 18th century:

> Laws and governments may be considered in this and indeed in every case, as a combination of the rich to oppress the poor, and preserve to themselves the inequality of the goods, which would otherwise be soon destroyed by the attacks of the poor, who if not hindered by the government would soon reduce the others to an equality with themselves by open violence.

The American colonists, having fought and won the war for independence from England, faced the question of what kind of government to establish. In 1786, three years after the treaty of peace was signed, there was a rebellion of farmers in western Massachusetts, led by Captain Daniel Shays, a veteran of the war. The uprising was crushed, but it put a scare into those leaders who were to become our Founding Fathers. After Shays Rebellion, General Henry Knox warned his former commander, George Washington, about the rebels:

> ...they see the weakness of government; they feel at once their own poverty, compared to the opulent and their own force, and they are determined to make use of the latter in order to remedy the former. Their creed is that the property of the U.S. has been protected from the confiscations of Britain by the Joint exertions of all, and therefore should be the common property of all.

The Constitutional Convention in Philadelphia for 1787 was called to deal with this problem, to set up "big government," to protect the interests of merchants, slaveholders, land speculators, to establish law and order and avert future rebellions like that of Shays.

When the debate took place in the various states over ratification of the Constitution, the Federalist Papers appeared in the New York press to support ratification. Federalist Paper #10, written by James Madison, made clear why a strong central government was needed, to curb the potential demand of a "majority faction" for "an equal division of property, or for any other improper or wicked object."

And so the Constitution set up big government, big enough to protect slaveholders against slave rebellion, to catch runaway slaves if they went from one state to another, to pay off bondholders, to pass tariffs on behalf of manufacturers, to tax poor farmers to pay for armies that would then attack the farmers if they resisted payment, as was done in the Whiskey Rebellion in Pennsylvania in 1794. Much of this was embodied in the legislation of the first Congress, responding to the request of the secretary of the Treasury, Alexander Hamilton.

For all of the nation's history, that legislative pattern was to continue. Government would defend the interests of the wealthy classes. It would raise tariffs higher and higher to help manufacturers, give subsidies to shipping interests, and a hundred million acres of land free to the railroads. It would use the armed forces to clear Indians off their land, to put down labor uprisings, to invade countries in the Caribbean for the benefit of American growers, bankers, investors. This was very big government.

When the Great Depression produced social turmoil, with strikes and protests all over the nation, the government responded with laws for social security (which one angry senator said would "take all the romance out of life"), unemployment insurance, subsidized housing, work programs, money for the arts. And in the atmosphere created by the movements of the Sixties, Medicare and Medicaid were enacted. Only then did the cry arise, among politicians and the press, continuing to this day, warning against "big government."

Of course, the alarms about "big government" did not extend to the enormous subsidies to business. When, after World War II, the aircraft industries, which had made enormous profits during the war (92% of their expansion paid for by the government), was in decline, Stuart Symington, Assistant Secretary of War for Air, wrote to the president of Aircraft Industries: "It looks as if our airplane industry is in trouble and it would seem to be the obligation of our little shop to do the best we can to help." The help came and has never stopped coming. Billions in subsidies each year to produce fighters and bombers.

When Chrysler ran out of cash in 1980, the government stepped in to help. (Try that next time you run out of cash.) Tax benefits, like the oil depletion allowance, added up over the years to hundreds of billions of dollars. For example, *The New York Times* reported in 1984 that the twelve top military contractors paid an average tax rate of 1.5% while middle-class Americans were paying 15% and more.

So it's time to gently point out the hypocrisy as both Democrats and Republicans decry "big government." When President Clinton signed the Crime Bill to build more federal prisons, when recently he called for billions more for the military budget, he did not refer to his campaign declaration that "the era of big government is over."

Surely, with only a bit of reflection, it becomes clear that the issue is not big or little government, but government for whom? Is it the ideal expressed by Lincoln—government "for the people," or is it the reality described by the Populist orator Mary Ellen Lease in 1890: "...a government of Wall Street, by Wall Street and for Wall Street."

There is good evidence that the American people, whose common sense often resists the most energetic propaganda campaigns, understand this. Political leaders and the press have pounded away at their sensibilities with the fearful talk of "big government," and so long as it is an abstraction, it is easy for people to go along, each listener defining it in his or her own way. But when specific questions are asked, the results are illuminating.

Again and again, public opinion surveys over the last decade have shown that people want the government to act to remedy economic injustice.

Last year, the Pew Research Center asked if it is "the responsibility of the government to take care of people who can't take care of themselves? Sixty-one percent said they either completely agreed or mostly agreed. When, after the Republican Congressional Victory in 1994 *The New York Times* asked people their opinions on "welfare," the responses were evenly for and against. The *Times* headline read: "PUBLIC SHOWS TRUST IN GOP CONGRESS," but this misled its readers, because when the question was posed more specifically: "Should the government help people in need?" over 65 percent answered in the affirmative.

This should not surprise us. The achievements of the New Deal programs still glow warmly in the public memory: social security, unemployment insurance, the work programs, the minimum wage, the subsidies for the arts. There is an initial worried reaction when people are confronted with the scare words "big government." But that falls away as soon as someone points to the G.I. Bill of Rights, Medicare, Medicaid, food stamps, and loans to small business.

So let's not hesitate to say: we want the government, responding to the Lincolnian definition of democracy, to organize, with the efficiency that it ran the G.I. Bill, that it runs Social Security and Medicare, a system that gives free medical care to everyone and pays for it out of a reformed tax system which is truly progressive. In short, we want everyone to be in the position of U.S. Senators, and members of the armed forces—beneficiaries of big, benevolent government.

"Big government" in itself is hardly the issue. That is here to stay. The only question is: whom will it serve?

10

Beyond Voting

The political culture of the United States is dominated by voting. Every election year is accompanied by an enormous amount of attention, with the media and the politicians joining forces to try to persuade Americans that voting for one candidate or another is the most important act of citizenship. I decided to challenge that idea in this column, which appeared in the *Boston Globe* at the start of the election campaign of 1976.

G ossip is the opium of the American public. We lie back, close our eyes and happily inhale the stories about Roosevelt's and Kennedy's affairs, Lyndon Johnson's nude swims with unnamed partners and, now, Nixon's pathetic "final days" in office.

The latest fix is administered by reporters Woodward and Bernstein and the stuff is Nixon's sex life with Pat, Nixon drunk and weeping, Nixon cradled in the arms of Kissinger (who did it, we presume, for national security).

So we get high on trivia, and forget that, whether Presidents have been impotent or oversexed, drunk or sober, they have followed the same basic policies. Whether crooks or Boy Scouts, handsome or homely, agile or clumsy, they have taxed the poor, subsidized the rich, wasted the wealth of the nation on guns and bombs, ignored the decay of the cities, and done so little for the children of the ghettos and rural wastelands that these youth had to join the armed forces to survive—until they were sent overseas to die.

Harry Truman was blunt and Lyndon Johnson wily, but both sent armies to Asia to defend dictators and massacre the people we claimed to be helping. Eisenhower was dull and Kennedy witty, but both built up huge nuclear armaments at the expense of schools and health care. Nixon was corrupt and Ford straightforward, but both coldly cut benefits for the poor and gave favors to rich corporations.

The cult of personality in America is a powerful drug. It takes the energy of ordinary citizens which, combined, can be a powerful force, and depletes it in the spectator sport of voting. Our most cherished moment of democratic citizenship comes when we leave the house once in four years to choose between two mediocre white Anglo-Saxon males who have been trundled out by political caucuses, million dollar primaries and managed conventions for the rigged multiple choice test we call an election. Presidents come and go. But the FBI is always there, on the job, sometimes catching criminals, sometimes committing crimes itself, always checking on radicals as secret police do all over the world. Its latest confession: ninety-two burglaries, 1960-66.

Presidents come and go, but the military budget keeps rising. It was $74 billion in 1973, is over $100 billion now (the equivalent of $2,000 in taxes for every family), and will reach $130 billion in 1980.

Presidents come and go, but the 200 top corporations keep increasing their control: 45 percent of all manufacturing in 1960, 60 percent by 1970.

No President in this century has stopped the trend. Not even FDR.

Yes, Roosevelt took steps to help poor people in the '30s. Minimum wages. Social security, WPA jobs. Relief. But that didn't change the basic nature of the capitalist system, whose highest priority has always been profits for the corporations and to hell with the rest.

Roosevelt was humane and wise, but, also, he had to react to signs of anger and rebellion in the country. He had seen the Bonus March of veterans to Washington under Hoover. In his first year, mass strikes—400,000 textile workers out in the South and New England. Longshoremen tied up the whole city of San Francisco. Teamsters took over Minneapolis. The unemployed were organizing, the bootleg miners taking over coalfields, tenants gathering in the cities to stop evictions.

Roosevelt was a sensitive man. But something big was happening in the country to sharpen his sensitivity.

1976: the multiple choice test is here again. Sure, there are better candidates and worse. But we will go a long way from spectator democracy to real democracy when we understand that the future of this country doesn't depend, mainly, on who is our next President. It depends on whether the American citizen, fed up with high taxes, high prices, unemployment, waste, war and corruption, will organize all over the country a clamor for change even greater than the labor uprisings of the '30s or the black rebellion of the '60s and shake this country out of old paths into new ones.

PART
3

On the
Holocaust

11

Respecting the Holocaust

There is perhaps no issue more emotionally provocative—to
Jews, but also to others—than the place of the Nazi Holocaust
in history. This essay in *The Progressive* brought a barrage of
responses, some positive, others critical. I leave it to readers to
make their own judgment.

Perhaps we—not just Jews but all who have taken seriously the
admonition "Never Again"—must ask ourselves, as we observe the
horrors around us in the world, if we have used that phrase as a beginning or as an ending to our moral concern.

Some years ago, when I was teaching at Boston University, I was
asked by a Jewish group to give a talk on the Holocaust. I spoke that
evening, but not about the Holocaust of World War II, not about the
genocide of six million Jews. It was the mid-Eighties, and the United
States government was supporting death squad governments in
Central America, so I spoke of the deaths of hundreds of thousands of
peasants in Guatemala and El Salvador, victims of American policy.

My point was that the memory of the Jewish Holocaust should

not be encircled by barbed wire, morally ghettoized, kept isolated from other genocides in history. It seemed to me that to remember what happened to Jews served no important purpose unless it aroused indignation, anger, action against all atrocities, anywhere in the world.

A few days later, in the campus newspaper, there was a letter from a faculty member who had heard me speak—a Jewish refugee who had left Europe for Argentina, and then the United States. He objected strenuously to my extending the moral issue from Jews in Europe in the 1940s to people in other parts of the world, in our time. The Holocaust was a sacred memory. It was a unique event, not to be compared to other events. He was outraged that, invited to speak on the Jewish Holocaust, I had chosen to speak about other matters.

I was reminded of this experience when I recently read a book by Peter Novick, *The Holocaust in American Life*. Novick's starting point is the question: why, fifty years after the event, does the Holocaust play a more prominent role in this country—the Holocaust Museum in Washington, hundreds of Holocaust programs in schools—than it did in the first decades after the second World War?

Surely at the core of the memory is a horror that should not be forgotten. But around that core, whose integrity needs no enhancement, there has grown up an industry of memorialists who have labored to keep that memory alive for purposes of their own.

Some Jews have used the Holocaust as a way of preserving a unique identity, which they see threatened by intermarriage and assimilation. Zionists have used the Holocaust, since the 1967 war, to justify further Israeli expansion into Palestinian land, and to build support for a beleaguered Israel (more beleaguered, as David Ben-Gurion had predicted, once it occupied the West Bank and Gaza). And non-Jewish politicians have used the Holocaust to build political support among the numerically small but influential Jewish voters—

note the solemn pronouncements of Presidents wearing yarmulkas to underline their anguished sympathy.

I would never have become a historian if I thought that it would become my professional duty to go into the past and never emerge, to study long-gone events and remember them only for their uniqueness, not connecting them to events going on in my time. If the Holocaust was to have any meaning, I thought, we must transfer our anger to the brutalities of our time. We must atone for our allowing the Jewish Holocaust to happen by refusing to allow similar atrocities to take place now—yes, to use the Day of Atonement not to pray for the dead but to act for the living, to rescue those about to die.

When Jews turn inward to concentrate on their own history, and look away from the ordeal of others, they are, with terrible irony, doing exactly what the rest of the world did in allowing the genocide to happen. There were shameful moments, travesties of Jewish humanism, as when Jewish organizations lobbied against a Congressional recognition of the Armenian Holocaust of 1915 on the ground that it diluted the memory of the Jewish Holocaust. The designers of the Holocaust Museum dropped the idea of mentioning the Armenian genocide after lobbying by the Israeli government. (Turkey was the only Moslem government with which Israel had diplomatic relations.)

Another such moment came when Elie Wiesel, chair of President Carter's Commission on the Holocaust, refused to include in a description of the Holocaust Hitler's killing of millions of non-Jews. That would be, he said, to "falsify" the reality "in the name of mis-guided universalism." Novick quotes Wiesel as saying, "They are steal-ing the Holocaust from us." As a result, the Holocaust Museum gave only passing attention to the five million or more non-Jews who died in the Nazi camps.

To build a wall around the uniqueness of the Jewish Holocaust is to abandon the idea that humankind is all one, that we are all, of whatever color, nationality, religion, deserving of equal rights to life, liberty, and the pursuit of happiness. What happened to the Jews under Hitler is unique in its details but it shares universal characteristics with many other events in human history: the Atlantic slave trade, the genocide against native Americans, the injuries and deaths to millions of working people, victims of the capitalist ethos that put profit before human life.

In recent years, while paying more and more homage to the Holocaust as a central symbol of man's cruelty to man, we have, by silence and inaction, collaborated in an endless chain of cruelties. Hiroshima and My Lai are the most dramatic symbols—and did we hear from Wiesel and other keepers of the Holocaust flame outrage against those atrocities? Langston Hughes once wrote (after the sentencing to death of the Scottsboro Boys): "Now, I thought, will the poets sing. But I have heard no cry. I wonder why."

There have been the massacres of Rwanda, and the starvation in Somalia, with our government watching and doing nothing. There were the death squads in Latin America, and the decimation of the population of East Timor, with our government actively collaborating. Our church-going Christian Presidents, so pious in their references to the genocide against the Jews, kept supplying the instruments of death to the perpetrators of other genocides.

True there are some horrors which seem beyond our powers. But there is an ongoing atrocity which is within our power to bring to an end. Novick points to it, and physician-anthropologist Paul Farmer describes it in detail in his remarkable book, *Infections and Inequalities*. That is: the deaths of ten million children all over the world who die every year of malnutrition and preventable diseases. The World Health Organization estimates three million people died last year of tuberculosis, which is preventable and curable, as Farmer has proved in his medical work in Haiti. With a small portion of our military budget we could wipe out tuberculosis.

The point of all this is not to diminish the experience of the Jewish Holocaust, but to enlarge it. For Jews it means to reclaim the tradition of Jewish universal humanism against an Israel-centered nationalism. Or, as Novick puts it, to go back to "that larger social consciousness that was the hallmark of the American Jewry of my youth." That larger consciousness was displayed in recent years by those Israelis who protested the beating of Palestinians in the Intifada, who demonstrated against the invasion of Lebanon.

For others—whether Armenians or Native Americans or Africans or Bosnians or whatever—it means to use their own bloody histories, not to set themselves against others, but to create a larger solidarity against the holders of wealth and power, the perpetrators and collaborators of the ongoing horrors of our time.

The Holocaust might serve a powerful purpose if it led us to think of the world today as wartime Germany—where millions die while the rest of the population obediently goes about its business. It is a frightening thought that the Nazis, in defeat, were victorious: today Germany, tomorrow the world. That is, until we withdraw our obedience.

PART 4

On Marxism

12

"Je Ne Suis Pas Marxiste"

For a long time I thought that there were important and useful ideas in Marxist philosophy and political economy that should be protected from the self-righteous cries on the right that "Marxism is dead," as well as from the arrogant assumptions of the commissars of various dictatorships that their monstrous regimes represented "Marxism." This piece was written for *Z Magazine*, June 1988, and reprinted in my book *Failure to Quit* (Common Courage Press, 1993).

Not long ago, someone referred to me publicly as a "Marxist professor." In fact, two people did. One was a spokesperson for "Accuracy in Academia," worried that there were "five thousand Marxist faculty members" in the United States (which diminished my importance, but also my loneliness). The other was a former student I encountered on a shuttle to New York, a fellow traveler. I felt a bit honored. A "Marxist" means a tough guy (making up for the pillowy connotation of "professor"), a person of formidable politics, someone not to be trifled with, someone who knows the difference between absolute and relative surplus value, and what is commodity fetishism, and refuses to buy it.

I was also a bit taken aback (a position which yoga practitioners understand well, and which is good for you about once a day). Did "Marxist" suggest that I kept a tiny statue of Lenin in my drawer and rubbed his head to discover what policy to follow to intensify the contradictions in the imperialist camp, or what songs to sing if we were sent away to such a camp?

Also, I remembered that famous statement of Marx: "Je ne suis pas Marxiste." I always wondered why Marx, an English-speaking German who had studied Greek for his doctoral dissertation, would make such an important statement in French. But I am confident that he did make it, and I think I know what brought it on. After Marx and his wife Jenny had moved to London, where they lost three of their six children to illness and lived in squalor for many years, they were often visited by a young German refugee named Pieper. This guy was a total "noodnik" (there are "noodniks" all along the political spectrum stationed ten feet apart, but there is a special Left Noodnik, hired by the police, to drive revolutionaries batty). Pieper (I swear, I did not make him up) hovered around Marx gasping with admiration, once offered to translate *Das Kapital* into English, which he could barely speak, and kept organizing Karl Marx Clubs, exasperating Marx more and more by insisting that every word Marx uttered was holy. And one day Marx caused Pieper to have a severe abdominal cramp when he said to him: "Thanks for inviting me to speak to your Karl Marx Club. But I can't. I'm not a Marxist."

That was a high point in Marx's life, and also a good starting point for considering Marx's ideas seriously without becoming a Pieper (or a Stalin, or a Kim II Sung, or any born-again Marxist who argues that every word in Volumes One, Two, and Three, and especially in the

Grundrisse, is unquestionably true). Because it seems to me (risking that this may lead to my inclusion in the second edition of Norman Podhoretz's *Register of Marxists, Living or Dead*), Marx had some very useful thoughts.

For instance, we find in Marx's short but powerful *Theses on Feuerbach* the idea that philosophers, who always considered their job was to interpret the world, should now set about changing it, in their writings, and in their lives.

Marx set a good example himself. While history has treated him as a sedentary scholar, spending all his time in the library of the British Museum, Marx was a tireless activist all his life. He was expelled from Germany, from Belgium, from France, was arrested and put on trial in Cologne.

Exiled to London, he kept his ties with revolutionary movements all over the world. The poverty-ridden flats that he and Jenny Marx and their children occupied became busy centers of political activity, gathering places for political refugees from the continent.

True, many of his writings were impossibly abstract (especially those on political economy; my poor head at the age of nineteen swam, or rather drowned, with ground rent and differential rent, the falling rate of profit and the organic composition of capital). But he departed from that constantly to confront the events of his time, to write about the revolutions of 1848, the Paris Commune, rebellion in India, the Civil War in the United States.

The manuscripts he wrote at the age of twenty-five while an exile in Paris (where he hung out in cafes with Engels, Proudhon, Bakunin, Heine, Stirner), often dismissed by hard-line fundamentalists as "immature," contain some of his most profound ideas. His critique of capitalism in those *Economic and Philosophic Manuscripts* did not need any mathematical proofs of "surplus value." It simply stated (but did not state it simply) that the capitalist system violates whatever it means to be human. The industrial system Marx saw developing in Europe not only robbed them of the product of their work, it estranged working people from their own creative possibilities, from one another as human beings, from the beauties of nature, from their own true selves. They lived out their lives not according to their own inner needs, but according to the necessities of survival.

This estrangement from self and others, this alienation from all that was human, could not be overcome by an intellectual effort, by something in the mind. What was needed was a fundamental, revolutionary change in society, to create the conditions—a short workday, a rational use of the earth's natural wealth and people's natural talents, a just distribution of the fruits of human labor, a new social consciousness—for the flowering of human potential, for a leap into freedom as it had never been experienced in history.

Marx understood how difficult it was to achieve this, because, no matter how "revolutionary" we are, the weight of tradition, habit, the accumulated mis-education of generations, "weighs like a nightmare on the brain of the living."

Marx understood politics. He saw that behind political conflicts were questions of class: who gets what. Behind benign bubbles of togetherness (*We* the people...*our* country...*national* security), the powerful and the wealthy would legislate on their own behalf. He noted (in *The Eighteenth Brumaire*, a biting, brilliant analysis of the Napoleonic seizure of power after the 1848 Revolution in France) how a modern constitution could proclaim absolute rights, which were then limited by marginal notes (he might have been predicting the tortured constructions of the First Amendment in our own Constitution), reflecting the reality of domination by one class over another regardless of the written word.

He saw religion, not just negatively as "the opium of the people," but positively as "the sigh of the oppressed creature, the heart of a heartless world, the soul of soulless conditions." This helps us under-stand the mass appeal of the religious charlatans of the television screen, as well as the work of Liberation Theology in joining the soul-fulness of religion to the energy of revolutionary movements in mis-erably poor countries.

Marx was often wrong, often dogmatic, often a "Marxist." He was sometimes too accepting of imperial domination as "progressive," a way of bringing capitalism faster to the third world, and therefore has-tening, he thought, the road to socialism. (But he staunchly support-ed the rebellions of the Irish, the Poles, the Indians, the Chinese, against colonial control.)

He was too insistent that the industrial working class must be the agent of revolution, and that this must happen first in the advanced capitalist countries. He was unnecessarily dense in his economic analyses (too much education in German universities, maybe) when his clear, simple insight into exploitation was enough: that no matter how valuable were the things workers produced, those who controlled the economy could pay them as little as they liked, and enrich them-selves with the difference.

Personally, Marx was sometimes charming, generous, self-sacrific-ing; at other times arrogant, obnoxious, abusive. He loved his wife and children, and they clearly adored him, but he also may have fathered the son of their German housekeeper, Lenchen.

The anarchist Bakunin, his rival in the International Workingmen's Association, said of Marx:

> I very much admired him for his knowledge and for his passionate and earnest devotion to the cause of the proletariat. But...our temperaments did not harmonize. He called me a sentimental idealist, and he was right. I called him vain, treacherous, and morose, and I was right.

Marx's daughter Eleanor, on the other hand, called her father

"...the cheeriest, gayest soul that ever breathed, a man brimming over with humor..."

He epitomized his own warning, that people, however advanced in their thinking, were weighted down by the limitations of their time. Still, Marx gave us acute insights, inspiring visions. I can't imagine Marx being pleased with the "socialism" of the Soviet Union. He would have been a dissident in Moscow, I like to think. His idea of the "dictatorship of the proletariat" was the Paris Commune of 1871, where endless argument in the streets and halls of the city gave it the vitality of a grass-roots democracy, where overbearing officials could be immediately booted out of office by popular vote, where the wages of government leaders could not exceed that of ordinary workers, where the guillotine was destroyed as a symbol of capital punishment. Marx once wrote in the *New York Tribune* that he did not see how capital punishment could be justified "in a society glorying in its civilization."

Perhaps the most precious heritage of Marx's thought is his internationalism, his hostility to the national state, his insistence that ordinary people have no nation they must obey and give their lives for in war, that we are all linked to one another across the globe as human beings. This is not only a direct challenge to modern capitalist nationalism, with its ugly evocations of hatred for "the enemy" abroad, and its false creation of a common interest for all within certain artificial borders. It is also a rejection of the narrow nationalism of contemporary "Marxist" states, whether the Soviet Union, or China, or any of the others.

Marx had something important to say not only as a critic of capitalism, but as a warning to revolutionaries, who, he wrote in *The German Ideology*, had better revolutionize themselves if they intended to do that to society. He offered an antidote to the dogmatists, the hard-liners, the Piepers, the Stalins, the commissars, the "Marxists." He said: "Nothing human is alien to me."

That seems a good beginning for changing the world.

13

The New Radicalism

By 1969 the civil rights movement and the anti-war movement had generated a huge amount of practical experience, without any obvious theoretical foundation. Priscilla Long thought it time to fill that gap. She assembled a set of essays in a book entitled *The New Left*, and it was put out by a small publisher in Boston, Porter Sargent. The introduction was written by historian and activist Staughton Lynd, and the very first essay was by someone generally acknowledged to be one of the intellectual mentors of the New Left, C. Wright Mills. The book included essays by Barbara Deming, Noam Chomsky, Daniel Berrigan, Paul Mattick, Percival and Paul Goodman. I wrote one called "Marxism and the New Left," which follows.

M y intention in this paper is not to define the radicalism of the New Left but to redefine it. By a remarkable coincidence, that is, I believe, in the spirit of Marxism—to declare what something *is* by declaring what it should be. Marxism assumes that everything— including an idea—takes on a new meaning in each additional moment of time, in each unique historical situation. It tries to avoid academic scholasticism, which pretends to dutifully record, to describe—forgetting that to merely describe is to circumscribe. (The pretense of passive description is what Herbert Marcuse in *One-Dimensional Man* called *operationalism.*)

Marxism is not a fixed body of dogma, to be put into big black books or little red books, and memorized, but a set of specific propositions about the modern world which are both tough and tentative, plus a certain vague and yet exhilarating vision of the future, and, more fundamentally, an approach to life, to people, to ourselves, a certain way of thinking about thinking as well as about being. Most of all it is a way of thinking which is intended to promote action.

The New Left—that loose amalgam of civil rights activists, Black Power advocates, ghetto organizers, student rebels, Vietnam protesters—has been exciting because it has been acting. In that circle of encounter where the spirit of Marxism and the action of the New Left intersect, the New Left will take from Marxism—if it is wise—not all of its exact propositions about the world Marx and Engels lived in (a world which is partly the same today and partly different), but its approach. This approach demands a constant redefinition of theory in the light of immediate reality, and an insistence on *action* as a way of both testing and reworking theory.

One of the most quoted, and most ignored, in practice, of Marx's statements is the eleventh point of his *Theses on Feuerbach* (about 1845): "The philosophers have only interpreted the world in various ways; the point however is to change it." Since any body of ideas is part of the world, this suggests our job is not merely to interpret Marxism and the New Left, but to change them. Earlier in these *Theses*, Marx criticized Feuerbach's emphasis on "the theoretical attitude." He said: "Social life is essentially practical. All mysteries...find their rational solution in human practice."

In their best moments, thinking revolutionaries agree with this.

When Mao Tse Tung was in Yenan, after the Long March, he gave his lecture "On Practice," where he talked of the primacy of experience in knowledge, of uniting perceptual knowledge with rational knowledge, rationalism with empiricism. He said: "The Marxist recognizes that in the absolute, total process of the development of the universe, the development of each concrete process is relative; hence in the great stream of absolute truth, man's knowledge of the concrete process at each given stage of development is only relatively true." That spirit is somehow different than what one encounters in the *Peking Review* these days, with its litany: Long Live Chairman Mao.

To try for a moment to act out the Marxist approach, look at the academic setting in which we live. We find that so much of what is called "intellectual history" is the aimless dredging up of what is and was, rather than a creative recollection of experience pointed at the betterment of human life. We are surrounded by solemn, pretentious argument about what Marx or Machiavelli or Rousseau really meant, about who was right and who was wrong—all of which is another way the pedant has of saying: "I am right and you are wrong." Too much of what passes for the theoretical discussion of public issues is really a personal duel for honor or privilege—with each discussant like the character in *Catch-22* who saw every event in the world as either a feather in his cap or a black eye—and this while men were dying all around him.

This scholasticism, oddly enough, has been typical both of the Old Left and of the academic journals, journals which would be horrified at being called Left or Right, and which indeed could hardly be accused of moving in any identifiable direction. Because the New Left is a successor to the Old Left in American history, and because it comes to a large extent out of the academic world (whether the Negro colleges of the South or the Berkeleys of the North), it is always being tempted by theoretical irrelevancies. Fortunately, the young people of today seem more nimble than their predecessors in avoiding this trap.

The contributions of the Old Left—and they were considerable—came not out of its ideological fetishism but out of its action. What gave it dynamism was not the classes on surplus value but the organization of the CIO, not the analysis of Stalin's views on the National and Colonial Question, but the fight for the Scottsboro boys, not the labored rationale for dictatorship of the proletariat, but the sacrifices of the Abraham Lincoln Battalion. I am not arguing here against theoretical discussion, or against long-range principles, or the analysis of sub-surface realities, but I am asserting that theory must be informed by observation and expressed in action. It must, in other words, be relevant.

A materialist approach—in the Marxian sense—makes suggestions rather than demands. One of these is that we look for the situational circumstances behind the behavior and thought of men, if we want to affect both. A dialectical approach—in the Marxian sense—suggests that we evaluate a situation not as fixed, but as in motion, and that our evaluation itself affects that motion. Dialectical materialism asks awareness that we are creatures of limited vision, in eyes and brain, and so must not assume that what we see or perceive is all—that conflicting tendencies often lie beneath the surface of any event.

These are not just academic observations: such an approach should make it easier for us to understand what is wrong when the government says to a penniless Negro in the Mississippi Delta, we have passed a bill and you are now free. Such an approach should help us to sense, in walking past the tenements of a city, temporarily quiet, the element of a violent insurrection. Marx's emphasis on the tyranny of economics can't tell us *how much* economic motivation there is behind any specific political act, but it can lead us to look for it. And so the New Left might go overboard in stressing economic interests in

Southeast Asia as an explanation for escalation in Vietnam—but it might be devilishly right in noting the connection between U.S. economic interests in Latin American nations and the pro-American votes of these nations in the U.N.

Marxism, in other words, doesn't tell us *exactly* what we will find beneath the surface—it does suggest that we should look for—and it certainly insists that we look. A Marxist would have given Lysenko his microscope; but it was a Stalinist who told him—or created an atmosphere that told him—what he must find beneath it.

And if someone says this isn't dialectical materialism or Marxism—this is common sense, or rationalism, or pragmatism, or empiricism, or naturalism—why deny that, or argue? Who cares about credit? True, the Old Left didn't like to admit relations with any other ideology. It remained virginal and lonely. The New Left seems different.

There has been much talk about a Christian-Marxist dialogue— but if such a dialogue is to be useful perhaps it should begin with the idea that God is dead and Marx is dead, but Yossarian lives. This is only a way of saying: let's not spend our time arguing whether God exists or what Marx really meant, because while we argue, the world moves, while we publish, others perish, and the best use of our energy is to resist those who would send us—after so many missions of murder—on still one more.

A new radicalism should be anti-ideological, I believe, in the sense I have discussed. But it also should be—and here it has been inadequate—concerned with theory. I see three essential ingredients in such a theory. First we need a vision of what we are working toward—one based on transcendental human needs and not limited by the reality we are so far stuck with. Second, this theory should analyze the present reality, not through the prism of old, fixed categories, but rather with an awareness of the unique here and now and of the need to make the present irrationality intelligible to those around us. Finally, such a theory would explore—in the midst of action—effective techniques of social change for the particular circumstances we find at the moment.

Let me speak now about the first requirement of this theory, the vision of the future. Here the Marxian vision is useful. True, it is vague. But what better guard is there against dogmatism than vagueness? Uncertainty is not a virtue in depicting the facts of the moment; it may not only be tolerable, but desirable, in trying to portray the future.

I stress this as a Marxian vision, even though many non-Marxists have held the same vision—because while it's necessary to emphasize to the Left that it does not monopolize either compassion or insight, it is necessary to remind everyone else—the Christians, the Jews, the Buddhists, the Humanists, and anyone else—that they share certain aims with Marxism. No one of these groups is going to revolutionize the world by itself, and so all need to be reminded of a certain consensus of humanistic values that has developed in the modern world. Marxists and liberals at their best (and they have not usually been at their best) share this theoretical consensus, here and abroad. Indeed, one of the great contributions of the New Left has been to remind both Marxist countries and liberal capitalist countries how far is their behavior from the values they claim.

In *The Holy Family*, one of the early writings of Marx and Engels (about 1845) they say man needs to be "not negatively free to avoid this or that event" but "positively free to express his true individuality." They say this requires arranging the empirical world around us so that "man experiences and assimilates there what is really human, that he experiences himself as a man." Rather than punishing individuals for their crimes, we should "destroy the social conditions which engender crime, and give to each individual the scope which he needs in society in order to develop his life." This speaks to the so-called socialist countries of today which imprison writers who criticize the state. It also speaks to a country like the United States, which gives people the negative freedoms of the Bill of Rights, but distributes very unequally the scope in which people can develop their individuality, can exercise their freedom—so that some children can roam in little suburban mansions surrounded by gardens, and others are equally free to play in rat-infested tenements. While every one "has" freedom of speech, the corporation with a million dollars to spend on television time can speak to thirty million people, and the individual who can afford a soap box can speak to thirty people. What makes the New Left so critical of the wealthiest nation in the world is its acute consciousness that freedom means not only legal permission to occupy space, but the resources to make the most of this.

The New Left has not even begun to figure out how to explain this complex problem of freedom to all those people in the United States brought up on high school history books and American Legion essay contests. What can make the New Radicalism really new, and really pertinent to here and now, is to be able, without recourse to the stale slogans about "bourgeois freedom," to do justice to the degree of freedom that does exist for people in the United States—while noting that it *is* a matter of degree, that freedom in America is like wealth, plentiful, and very unequally distributed.

Let me turn to another element in the Marxian vision. There is still a widespread popular belief, heavily stressed on the *Reader's Digest* level, that Marxism believes in the supremacy of the state over the individual, while democracy believes the opposite. In fact, the existence of oppressively overbearing states in the world, which call themselves Marxist, reinforces this idea. But a true radicalism would remind people in both socialist and capitalist countries of Marx's and Engels' hope, expressed early in the *Manifesto*, that some day "the public power will lose its political character" and "we shall have an association in which the free development of each is the condition for the free development of all." This is not just a youthful aberration (there is a fad about the young romantic Marx and the old, practical Marx) because twenty-seven years later, Marx, in his *Critique of the Gotha Program*, says: "Freedom consists in converting the state from an organ superimposed upon society into one completely subordinate to it." Here also he says, on the subject of the state giving education to the people, "the state has need, on the contrary, of a very stern education by the people." And Engels, a year after Marx's death, in 1884, writes in his *Origin of the Family, Private Property and the State:*

> The society that will organize production on the basis of a free and equal association of the producers will put the whole machinery of state where it will then belong: into the musum of antiquities, by the side of the spinning wheel and the bronze ax.

Their attitude to the state is made even clearer and more specific in Marx's book on the *Civil War in France*, and Engels' *Introduction* to it, where, both of them point admiringly to the Paris Commune of early 1871. The Commune almost immediately abolished conscription and the standing army, declared universal suffrage and the right of citizens to recall their elected officials at any time, said all officials, high or low, should be paid the same wage as received by other workers, and publicly burned the guillotine.

The New Left is anti-authoritarian; it would—I expect—burn draft cards in any society. It is anarchistic not just in wanting the ultimate abolition of the state, but in its immediate requirement that authority and coercion be banished in every sphere of existence, that the end must be represented immediately in the means. Marx and Bakunin disagreed on this, but the New Left has the advantage over Marx of having an extra century of history to study. We see how a dictatorship of the proletariat can easily become a dictatorship over the proletariat, as Trotsky warned, as Rosa Luxemburg warned. The New Left should remind the socialist states as well as the capitalist states of Marx's letter of 1853 to the *New York Tribune* saying he didn't know how capital punishment could be justified "in a society glorying in its civilization."

In America, both liberalism and radicalism were beguiled into cheering for state power because under FDR it seemed beneficent: it enacted certain economic reforms, and it waged war against Hitler. The New Left, hopefully, will recognize that the state cannot be trusted, either to carry reforms far enough, or to drop bombs only on Nazi invaders and not on Asian peasants in their own country. It will therefore create constellations of power outside the state to pressure it into humane actions, to resist its inhumane actions, and to replace it in many functions by voluntary small groups seeking to maintain both individuality and co-operation. Black Power, in its best aspects, is such an endeavor.

The New Left in America needs to show people how the state, whether a proletarian dictatorship or a sophisticated welfare capitalism, constitutes a special interest of its own which deserves not unthinking loyalty, but criticism, resistance, and (even in its better moments) watchfulness. This New Left attitude toward the state expresses a more general attitude—against making instruments into absolutes or means into ends—against the deification of any party, any nation, any ideology, any method.

Now another point about the Marxian vision. Perhaps nowhere does Marx speak more directly to our mass society today, and therefore to the new radicals in mass society, than in his *Economic and Philosophical Manuscripts* of 1844. The estrangement of man described there is pertinent not only to the classical proletariat of his time but to all classes in every modern industrial society—and certainly to the young people of this generation in the Untied States. He talks of men producing things alien to themselves, which become monsters independent of them (look all around us, at our automobiles, our television sets, our skyscrapers, even our universities). People find no satisfaction in working. He points to the irony that in man's specifically human functions (working, creating) he feels like an animal, while only in his animal functions (eating, sex) does he feel like a human being. Our activity becomes not enjoyable in itself, but just means to keep alive. Activity *is* life—what else is life?—and yet it becomes in modern society only a means to life.

So, we become estranged from what we produce, from our own activity, from our fellow men, from nature (here Marxism must share credit with Taoism), and finally from ourselves—because we all find ourselves living another life, not the one we really want to live. The New Radicals of today are desperately conscious of this and try to escape it. They want to do work which is congenial to them—so they go to Mississippi or move into the ghetto—or they don't work at all rather than work at hateful or parasitic jobs. They often try to create relationships with one another which are not warped by the rules and demands of the world around them. The crucial cause of all these forms of estrangement is that people's activities are coerced rather than free, and so the young people today are defiant. Living differently is not easy, but the very act of attempting it is a free act.

From all this it is quite clear what Marx's values were; the free man, in his individuality, in his sociality, in his oneness with nature. The New Left is in accord here. Where it parts, I think, is in Marx's claim—although some attribute this to Engels (one of those academic disputes I spoke about) that this vision of unalienated man springs not from a wish, but from an observation—from a scientific plotting of a historical curve which moves inevitably in the direction of man's freedom.

Surely we don't have such confidence in inevitabilities these days—we've had too many surprises in this century. (Simone de Beauvoir says in her book *The Ethics of Antiquity* that there is no inevitable proletarian uprising—the movement may go in six different directions.) We are unabashed in declaring our subjective wants and desires—without needing a "scientific" basis for such wants. Here again, the discussion of whether ethical norms are grounded in empirical science is one of those academic discussions which lead us nowhere in actuality. Surely, most people agree on the gross necessities of life—food, sex, peace, freedom, love, dignity, self-realization. Our energy should be spent in working toward them, not in discussing their metaphysical meaning.

I suggested above that the second requirement of a pertinent theory is an analysis of the *particulars* of today's reality. One of Marx's great perceptions was that there is a material basis for man's alienation and unhappiness—the scarcity of goods which he and society need, producing conflict, exploitation, coercion. Thus, abundance is a prerequisite—thought not a guarantee—of man's freedom. In the United States, we face this paradox, that the state with the most enormous productive apparatus, indeed the only state in the world which has the technological capacity to have communism, and where a communist society would have the greatest chance of preserving the freedom of the individual (because the *socialist* societies are plagued by scarcity) gets apoplectic at the very mention of the word.

It is here in the United States that the slogan "to each according to his need" can have meaning. We have enough doctors and hospitals to give adequate medical care to whoever needs it, without rationing this according to wealth. We grow enough food in this country without insisting that people without money do with very little food. We can—if we want to—built enough homes in this country to eliminate slums. And so on. There is room for some scholarly work here: economists could sit down somewhere and work out a specific plan for free food in America, also for free college tuition and allowances. What the New Left needs to show, and in specific detail, is where the resources are in this country, what they *are* being used for, and what they *could* be used for.

The Marxian economic categories have long provided material for academic controversy—and I doubt that Marx intended this. But he was only human and perhaps he too succumbed to the temptations of the intellectual: his research, his curiosity, his passion for scheme-building and for scientific constructions ran away with him. I confess that I cannot see how his dense Volume II of *Das Kapital* on the "Circulation of Commodities" or his long expositions of absolute rent and differential rent are essential to revolutionary theory. Does it really matter if Böhm-Bawerk was right or wrong on the relationship between aggregate surplus value and aggregate prices of production?

Even so brilliant a theory as that of surplus-value—how relevant is it to social action? Has the militancy of workingmen in history required such an analysis to sustain it? Has such militancy been transformed into revolutionary consciousness anywhere by the comprehension of the distinction between the use value and exchange value of labor power? The Baran-Sweezy notion of a surplus (in *Monopoly Capital*) comprised of waste, military expenses, and unused capacity, is more fruitful, I think, as a theoretical prod to revolutionary action.

James Bevel is right when he says you can only organize large numbers of people around issues that are obvious or that can easily be made obvious. So instead of discussing the falling rate of profit, or the organic composition of capital, I would concentrate on what is readily observable—that this country has enormous resources which it wastes shamefully and distributes unjustly. A country that produces 200 billion dollars worth of goods and services a year, and this is not our full capacity, should not have ten million families living below the

$3,000 a year level. All the Chamber of Commerce pronouncements, the fancy *Fortune Magazine* charts about our progress, the confident State of the Union Addresses, fall apart when you take a long walk through any major American city: through Harlem or Roxbury or Chicago's South Side.

The most useful Marxian statement about capitalist society is the largest one—that in an era when production is a complex, world-wide social process, and requires rationality, our system is incredibly irrational. This is because corporate profit, not human need, governs what is produced and what is not produced. It is also because there is a huge vested interest—economic, military, political, psychological—in the production of present and future corpses, on which we spend seventy billion dollars a year. We spend about twenty billion dollars a year on public relations, advertising, promotion. We build too many cars, too many highways, too many office buildings, produce too many cigarettes, too much liquor, too many gadgets and not enough homes, schools, hospitals. Corporate profits after taxes amount to forty billion dollars a year—enough to raise every $3,000 a year family to $7,000 a year. The New Left, instead of getting involved in theoretical discussions about economic categories, needs to find ways to make clear to Americans how wasteful, irrational, and unjust is our economy.

With a vision of how man should live, with some perception of how men do live (and so many of us need to be *shown*), the most urgent theoretical problem for the New Left—and the one where traditional Marxism gives the least guidance—is: how do we change society? How do we redistribute the power in society in order to redistribute the wealth? How do we overcome those who are enjoying power and wealth and won't give it up? How do we stop the fanaticism of both civilian and military leaders who feel it is America's duty to establish its power, or its puppets, wherever possible in the world—and don't care how many people, Americans or others—they kill in the process?

The traditional Marxian idea of a revolution taking place because of a breakdown in the capitalist mechanism and an organized, class-conscious proletariat taking over, is hardly tenable today. Where socialist revolutions have taken place in the world, they have taken place mostly because war has weakened or destroyed the state and created a vacuum in which organized revolutionaries could take over. The traditional liberal idea of a gradual evolution towards freedom, peace, and democracy through parliamentary reform is also hardly tenable. We see that poverty and racism can be institutionalized, with only token steps taken to assuage their worst aspects; that by creating a contended, bloated middle class, by introducing state regulatory mechanisms in the economy, the *status quo* can be maintained. And furthermore, in foreign policy, it has become accepted that the President and a small group of advisers make foreign policy, while the mass communications industry creates a nation of sheep who give assent.

Certainly, in the United States, the traditional idea that the agent of social change will be the proletariat needs re-examination, when the best-organized of the workers are bribed into silence with suburban houses and automobiles, and drugged into compliance with mass entertainment. Perhaps unorganized workers—the bulk of the labor force—may play a part, but these consist of white collar workers, domestic workers, migratory and farm laborers, service industry workers, and various kinds of people who are the hardest to organize. Recent experience suggests that Negroes—and perhaps Negroes in the ghetto—may be the most powerful single force for social change in the United States. Marx envisioned the industrial proletariat as the revolutionary agent because it was in need, exploited, and brought face to face in the factory. The Negro is in need, exploited and brought together in the ghetto. And since Berkeley and the teach-ins, there is some evidence that students—especially as they are pushed more and more toward the mouth of the cannon—may be another important agent of change. Perhaps some peculiar combination, unpredictable at this moment, will be formed in a time of national crisis.

How will change come about? By tactics short of violent revolution, but far more militant than normal parliamentary procedure, it seems to me. Even the demonstrations of the civil rights movement were not enough to achieve more than tokens of change: a few laws, a few high appointments, and LBJ reciting "We Shall Overcome." Spontaneous uprisings in the ghetto are alarm signals, but do not produce change in themselves. It will take systematic, persistent organizing and education, in the ghettos, in the universities, plus co-ordinated actions of various kinds designed to shock society out of its lethargy.

The New Left's idea of parallel organizations, as a way of *demonstrating* what people should do, how people should live, has enormous possibilities: freedom schools, free universities, free cities—remember how these grew up in medieval times outside the feudal system—self-controlled communities. But also, free, active *pockets* of people inside the traditional cities, universities, corporations. In military combat, guerrilla warfare arose as an answer to overwhelmingly centralized military power. Perhaps we are in need of political guerrilla tactics in the face of mass society—in which enclaves of freedom are created here and there in the midst of the orthodox way of life, to become centers of protest, and examples to others. It is in techniques of organization, pressure, change, community-building—that the New Radicals need the most thought, and the most action. It may take an ingenious combination of energy and wit to carry through a new kind of revolution.

Action *is* preferably organized, thought-out action, but there should be room for whatever kinds of action any individual or group feels moved to undertake. In an era when it is so easy to feel helpless, we need the Existentialist emphasis on our freedom to act. The

Marxist-Existentialist debate on freedom and determinism seems to me to be an empty one—an academic one. To stress our freedom is not the result of ignorance that we do have a history, that we do have an oppressive environment. But knowing of these pressures on us, we should be existentially aware that there is enormous indeterminacy in the combat between us and the obstacles all around. We never know exactly the depth or the shallowness of the resistance to our actions— until we act. We never know exactly what effect we will have. Our actions may lead to nothing except changing ourselves, and that is something. They may have a tiny cumulative effect, along with a thousand other actions. They may also explode.

What the fact of indeterminacy suggests is that we should not be preoccupied with prediction or with measuring immediate success— but rather should take the risk of acting. We are not totally free but our strength will be maximized if we act *as if* we are free. We are not passive observers, students, theorizers; our very thoughts, our statements, our speeches, our essays, throw a weight into a balance which cannot be assessed until we act. This Existentialist emphasis on the necessity for action—based on conscience, avoiding that cool and careful weighing of "the realities"—is one of the most refreshing characteristics of the New Radicalism in America.

Along with the Existentialist emphasis on freedom there is responsibility. To the extent that we feel free, we feel responsible. There is something about our time which makes it difficult for us not only to feel free but to feel responsibility. Contemporary life is complicated, and evil comes at the end of a long assembly line with a division of labor so intricate it is impossible to trace; everyone has responsibility and no one has responsibility. But if we are to feel our own freedom, we must feel our responsibility, not for anyone else's actions, but only for our own; not for the past and without any pledge to the future— but at this moment, now where we stand.

PART 5

On the Role
of the
Historian

14

Columbus and
Western Civilization

In the year 1992, the celebration of Columbus Day was different
from previous ones in two ways. First, this was the quincentennial, five hundred years after Columbus' landing in this hemisphere. Second, it was a celebration challenged all over the
country by people—many of them native Americans but also
others—who had "discovered" a Columbus not worth celebrating, and who were rethinking the traditional glorification of
"Western civilization." I gave this talk at the University of
Wisconsin in Madison in October of 1991. It was published the
following year by the Open Magazine Pamphlet Series with the
title "Christopher Columbus & The Myth of Human Progress."

George Orwell, who was a very wise man, wrote: "Who controls
the past controls the future. And who controls the present controls the past." In other words, those who dominate our society are in
a position to write our histories. And if they can do that, they can

decide our futures. That is why the telling of the Columbus story is important.

Let me make a confession. I knew very little about Columbus until about 12 years ago, when I began writing my book *A People's History of the United States*. I had a Ph.D. in history from Columbia University—that is, I had the proper training of a historian, and what I knew about Columbus was pretty much what I had learned in elementary school.

But when I began to write my *People's History*, I decided I must learn about Columbus. I had already concluded that I did not want to write just another overview of American history—I knew my point of view would be different. I was going to write about the United States from the point of view of those people who had been largely neglected in the history books: the indigenous Americans, the black slaves, the women, the working people, whether native or immigrant.

I wanted to tell the story of the nation's industrial progress from the standpoint, not of Rockefeller and Carnegie and Vanderbilt, but of the people who worked in their mines, their oil fields, who lost their limbs or their lives building the railroads.

I wanted to tell the story of wars, not from the standpoint of generals and presidents, not from the standpoint of those military heroes whose statues you see all over this country, but through the eyes of the GIs, or through the eyes of "the enemy." Yes, why not look at the Mexican War, that great military triumph of the United States, from the viewpoint of the Mexicans?

And so, how must I tell the story of Columbus? I concluded, I must see him through the eyes of the people who were here when he arrived, the people he called "Indians" because he thought he was in Asia.

Well, they left no memoirs, no histories. Their culture was an oral culture, not a written one. Besides, they had been wiped out in a few decades after Columbus' arrival. So I was compelled to turn to the next best thing: the Spaniards who were on the scene at the time. First, Columbus himself. He had kept a journal.

His journal was revealing. He described the people who greeted him when he landed in the Bahamas—they were Arawak Indians, sometimes called Tainos—and told how they waded out into the sea to greet him and his men, who must have looked and sounded like people from another world, and brought them gifts of various kinds. He described them as peaceable, gentle, and said: "They do not bear arms, and do not know them for I showed them a sword—they took it by the edge and cut themselves."

Throughout his journal, over the next months, Columbus spoke of the native Americans with what seemed like admiring awe:

> They are the best people in the world and above all the gentlest—without knowledge of what is evil—nor do they murder or steal...they love their neighbors as themselves and they have the sweetest talk in the world...always laughing.

And in a letter he wrote to one of his Spanish patrons, Columbus said:

> They are very simple and honest and exceedingly liberal with all they have, none of them refusing anything he may possess when he is asked for it. They exhibit great love toward all others in preference to themselves.

But then, in the midst of all this, in his journal, Columbus writes:

> They would make fine servants. With fifty men we could subjugate them all and make them do whatever we want.

Yes, this was how Columbus saw the Indians—not as hospitable hosts, but as "servants," to "do whatever we want."

And what did Columbus want? This is not hard to determine. In the first two weeks of journal entries, there is one word that recurs seventy-five times: GOLD.

In the standard accounts of Columbus what is emphasized again and again is his religious feeling, his desire to convert the natives to Christianity, his reverence for the Bible. Yes, he was concerned about God. But more about Gold. Just one additional letter. His was a limited alphabet. Yes, all over the island of Hispaniola, where he, his brothers, his men, spent most of their time, he erected crosses. But also, all over the island, they built gallows—340 of them by the year 1,500. Crosses and gallows—that deadly historic juxtaposition.

In his quest for gold, Columbus, seeing bits of gold among the Indians, concluded there were huge amounts of it. He ordered the natives to find a certain amount of gold within a certain period of time. And if they did not meet their quota, their arms were hacked off. The others were to learn from this and deliver the gold.

Samuel Eliot Morison, the Harvard historian who was Columbus' admiring biographer, acknowledged this. He wrote:

> Whoever thought up this ghastly system, Columbus was responsible for it, as the only means of producing gold for export.... Those who fled to the mountains were hunted with hounds, and of those who escaped, starvation and disease took toll, while thousands of the poor creatures in desperation took cassava poison to end their miseries.
>
> So the policy and acts of Columbus for which he alone was responsible began the depopulation of the terrestrial paradise that was Hispaniola in 1492. Of the original natives, estimated by a modern ethnologist at 300,000 in number, one-third were killed off between 1494 and 1496. By 1508, an enumeration showed only 60,000 alive...in 1548 Oviedo [Morison is referring to Fernandez de Oviedo, the official Spanish historian of the conquest] doubted whether 500 Indians remained.

But Columbus could not obtain enough gold to send home to impress the King and Queen and his Spanish financiers, so he decided to send back to Spain another kind of loot: slaves. They rounded up about 1,200 natives, selected 500, and these were sent, jammed together, on the voyage across the Atlantic. Two hundred died on the way, of cold, of sickness.

In Columbus' journal, an entry of September 1498 reads: "From here one might send, in the name of the Holy Trinity, as many slaves as could be sold..."

What the Spaniards did to the Indians is told in horrifying detail by Bartolomé de las Casas, whose writings give the most thorough account of the Spanish-Indian encounter. Las Casas was a Dominican priest who came to the New World a few years after Columbus, spent forty years on Hispaniola and nearby islands, and became the leading advocate in Spain for the rights of the natives. Las Casas, in his book *The Devastation of the Indies*, writes of the Arawaks:

> ...of all the infinite universe of humanity, these people are the most guile-less, the most devoid of wickedness and duplicity...yet into this sheep-fold...there came some Spaniards who immediately behaved like ravening beasts.... Their reason for killing and destroying...is that the Christians have an ultimate aim which is to acquire gold...

The cruelties multiplied. Las Casas saw soldiers stabbing Indians for sport, dashing babies' heads on rocks. And when the Indians resisted, the Spaniards hunted them down, equipped for killing with horses, armor plate, lances, pikes, rifles, crossbows, and vicious dogs. Indians who took things belonging to the Spaniards—they were not accustomed to the concept of private ownership and gave freely of their own possessions—were beheaded, or burned at the stake.

Las Casas' testimony was corroborated by other eyewitnesses. A group of Dominican friars, addressing the Spanish monarchy in 1519, hoping for the Spanish government to intercede, told about unspeakable atrocities, children thrown to dogs to be devoured, new-born babies born to women prisoners flung into the jungle to die.

Forced labor in the mines and on the land led to much sickness and death. Many children died because their mothers, overworked and starved, had no milk for them. Las Casas, in Cuba, estimated that 7000 children died in *three months.*

The greatest toll was taken by sickness, because the Europeans brought with them diseases against which the natives had no immunity: typhoid, typhus, diphtheria, smallpox.

As in any military conquest, women came in for especially brutal treatment. One Italian nobleman named Cuneo recorded an early sexual encounter. The "Admiral" he refers to is Columbus, who, as part of his agreement with the Spanish monarchy, insisted he be made an Admiral. Cuneo wrote:

> ...I captured a very beautiful Carib woman, whom the said Lord Admiral gave to me and with whom...I conceived desire to take pleasure. I wanted to put my desire into execution but she did not want it and treated me with her finger nails in such a manner that I wished I had never begun. But seeing that, I took a rope and thrashed her well.... Finally we came to an agreement."

There is other evidence which adds up to a picture of widespread rape of native women. Samuel Eliot Morison wrote: "In the Bahamas, Cuba and Hispaniola they found young and beautiful women, who everywhere were naked, in most places accessible, and presumably complaisant." Who presumes this? Morison, and so many others.

Morison saw the conquest as so many writers after him have done, as one of the great romantic adventures of world history. He seemed to get carried away by what appeared to him as a *masculine* conquest. He wrote:

"Never again may mortal men hope to recapture the amazement, the wonder, the delight of those October days in 1492, when the new world gracefully yielded her virginity to the conquering Castilians."

The language of Cuneo ("we came to an agreement"), and of Morison ("gracefully yielded") written almost five hundred years apart, surely suggests how persistent through modern history has been the mythology that rationalizes sexual brutality by seeing it as "complaisant."

So, I read Columbus' journal, I read Las Casas. I also read Hans Koning's pioneering work of our time—*Columbus: His Enterprise,* which, at the time I wrote my *People's History* was the only contemporary account I could find which departed from the standard treatment.

When my book appeared, I began to get letters from all over the country about it. Here was a book of 600 pages, starting with Columbus, ending with the 1970s, but most of the letters I got from readers were about one subject: Columbus. I could have interpreted this to mean that, since this was the very beginning of the book, that's all these people had read. But no, it seemed that the Columbus story was simply the part of my book that readers found most startling. Because every American, from elementary school on, learns the Columbus story, and learns it the same way: "In Fourteen Hundred and Ninety Two, Columbus Sailed the Ocean Blue."

How many of you have heard of Tigard, Oregon? Well, I didn't, until, about seven years ago, I began receiving, every semester, a bunch of letters, twenty or thirty, from students at one high school in Tigard, Oregon. It seems that their teacher was having them (knowing high schools, I almost said "forcing them") read my *People's History.* He was photocopying a number of chapters and giving them to the students. And then he had them write letters to me, with comments and questions. Roughly half of them thanked me for giving them data which they had never seen before. The others were angry, or wondered how

I got such information, and how I had arrived at such outrageous conclusions.

One high school student named Bethany wrote: "Out of all the articles that I've read of yours I found 'Columbus, The Indians, and Human Progress' the most shocking." Another student named Brian, seventeen years old, wrote: "An example of the confusion I feel after reading your article concerns Columbus coming to America.... According to you, it seems he came for women, slaves, and gold. You say that Columbus physically abused the Indians that didn't help him find gold. You've said you have gained a lot of this information from Columbus' own journal. I am wondering if there is such a journal, and if so, why isn't it part of our history. Why isn't any of what you say in my history book, or in history books people have access to each day."

I pondered this letter. It could be interpreted to mean that the writer was indignant that no other history books had told him what I did. Or, as was more likely, he was saying: "I don't believe a word of what you wrote! You made this up!"

I am not surprised at such reactions. It tells something about the claims of pluralism and diversity in American culture, the pride in our "free society," that generation after generation has learned exactly the same set of facts about Columbus, and finished their education with the same glaring omissions.

A school teacher in Portland, Oregon named Bill Bigelow has undertaken a crusade to change the way the Columbus story is taught all over America. He tells of how he sometimes starts a new class. He goes over to a girl sitting in the front row, and takes her purse. She says: "You took my purse!" Bigelow responds: "No, I discovered it."

Bill Bigelow did a study of recent children's books on Columbus. He found them remarkably alike in their repetition of the traditional point of view. A typical fifth grade biography of Columbus begins: "There once was a boy who loved the salty sea." Well! I can imagine a children's biography of Attila the Hun beginning with the sentence: "There once was a boy who loved horses."

Another children's book in Bigelow's study, this time for second graders:

> The King and queen looked at the gold and the Indians. They listened in wonder to Columbus' stories of adventure. Then they all went to church to pray and sing. Tears of joy filled Columbus' eyes.

I once spoke about Columbus to a workshop of school teachers, and one of them suggested that school children were too young to hear of the horrors recounted by Las Casas and others. Other teachers disagreed, said children's stories include plenty of violence, but the perpetrators are witches and monsters and "bad people," not national heroes who have holidays named after them.

Some of the teachers made suggestions on how the truth could be told in a way that would not frighten children unnecessarily, but that would avoid the falsification of history now taking place.

The arguments about children "not being ready to hear the truth" does not account for the fact that in American society, when the children grow up, they *still* are not told the truth. As I said earlier, right up through graduate school I was not presented with the information that would counter the myths told to me in the early grades. And it is clear that my experience is typical, judging from the shocked reactions to my book that I have received from readers of all ages.

If you look in an *adult* book, the *Columbia Encyclopedia* (my edition was put together in 1950, but all the relevant information was available then, including Morison's biography), there is a long entry on Columbus (about 1,000 words) but you will find no mention of the atrocities committed by him and his men.

In the 1986 edition of the *Columbia History of the World,* there are several mentions of Columbus, but nothing about what he did to the natives. Several pages are devoted to "Spain and Portugal in America," in which the treatment of the native population is presented as a matter of controversy, among theologians at that time, and among historians today. You can get the flavor of this "balanced approach," containing a nugget of reality, by the following passage from that *History:*

> The determination of the Crown and the Church to Christianize the Indians, the need for labor to exploit the new lands, and the attempts of some Spaniards to protect the Indians, resulted in a very remarkable complex of customs, laws, and institutions which even today leads historians to contradictory conclusions about Spanish rule in America.... Academic disputes flourish on this debatable and in a sense insoluble question, but there is no doubt that cruelty, overwork and disease resulted in an appalling depopulation. There were, according to recent estimates, about 25 million Indians in Mexico in 1519, slightly more than 1 million in 1605.

Despite this scholarly language—"contradictory conclusions...academic disputes...insoluble question"—there is no real dispute about the facts of enslavement, forced labor, rape, murder, the taking of hostages, the ravages of diseases carried from Europe, and the wiping out of huge numbers of native people. The only dispute is over how much emphasis is to be placed on these facts, and how they carry over into the issues of our time.

For instance, Samuel Eliot Morison does spend some time detailing the treatment of the natives by Columbus and his men, and uses the word "genocide" to describe the overall effect of the "discovery." But he buries this in the midst of a long, admiring treatment of Columbus, and sums up his view in the concluding paragraph of his popular book *Christopher Columbus, Mariner,* as follows:

> He had his faults and his defects, but they were largely the defects of the qualities that made him great—his indomitable will, his superb faith in God and in his own mission as the Christ-bearer to lands beyond the seas, his stubborn persistence despite neglect, poverty and discouragement. But

there was no flaw, no dark side to the most outstanding and essential of all his qualities—his seamanship.

Yes, his seamanship!

Let me make myself clear. I am not interested in either denouncing or exalting Columbus. It is too late for that. We are not writing a letter of recommendation for him to decide his qualifications for undertaking another voyage to another part of the universe. To me, the Columbus story is important for what it tells us about ourselves, about our time, about the decisions we have to make for our century, for the next century.

Why this great controversy today about Columbus and the celebration of the quincentennial? Why the indignation of native Americans and others about the glorification of that conqueror? Why the heated defense of Columbus by others? The intensity of the debate can only be because it is not about 1492, it is about 1992.

We can get a clue to this if we look back a hundred years to 1892, the year of the quadricentennial. There were great celebrations in Chicago and New York. In New York there were five days of parades, fireworks, military marches, naval pageants, a million visitors to the city, a memorial statue unveiled at a corner of Central Park, now to be known as Columbus Circle. A celebratory meeting took place at Carnegie Hall, addressed by Chauncey DePew.

You might not know the name of Chauncey DePew, unless you recently looked at Gustavus Myers' classic work, *A History of the Great American Fortunes*. In that book, Chauncey DePew is described as the front man for Cornelius Vanderbilt and his New York Central railroad. DePew traveled to Albany, the capital of New York State, with satchels of money and free railroad passes for members of the New York State legislature, and came away with subsidies and land grants for the New York Central.

DePew saw the Columbus festivities as a celebration of wealth and prosperity—you might say, as a self-celebration. He said that the quadricentennial event "marks the wealth and the civilization of a great people...it marks the things that belong to their comfort and their ease, their pleasure and their luxuries...and their power."

We might note that at the time he said this, there was much suffering among the working poor of America, huddled in city slums, their children sick and undernourished. The plight of people who worked on the land—which at this time was a considerable part of the population—was desperate, leading to the anger of the Farmers' Alliances and the rise of the People's (Populist) Party. And the following year, 1893 was a year of economic crisis and widespread misery.

DePew must have sensed, as he stood on the platform at Carnegie Hall, some murmurings of discontent at the smugness that accompanied the Columbus celebrations, for he said:

> If there is anything I detest...it is that spirit of historical inquiry which
> doubts everything; that modern spirit which destroys all the illusions and
> all the heroes which have been the inspiration of patriotism through all the
> centuries.

So, to celebrate Columbus was to be patriotic. To doubt was to be unpatriotic. And what did "patriotism" mean to DePew? It meant the glorification of expansion and conquest—which Columbus represented, and which America represented. It was just six years after his speech that the United States, expelling Spain from Cuba, began its own long occupation (sporadically military, continuously political and economic) of Cuba, took Puerto Rico and Hawaii, and began its bloody war against the Filipinos to take over their country.

That "patriotism" which was tied to the celebration of Columbus, and the celebration of conquest, was reinforced in the second World War by the emergence of the United States as the superpower, all the old European empires now in decline. At that time, Henry Luce, the powerful president-maker and multi-millionaire, owner of *Time, Life,* and *Fortune* (not just the publications, but the *things!*) wrote that the twentieth century was turning into the "American Century," in which the United States would have its way in the world.

George Bush, accepting the presidential nomination in 1988, said: "This has been called the American Century because in it we were the dominant force for good in the world.... Now we are on the verge of a new century, and what country's name will it bear? I say it will be another American Century."

What arrogance! That the twenty-first century, when we should be getting away from the murderous jingoism of this century, should already be anticipated as an *American* century, or as any one nation's century. Bush must think of himself as a new Columbus, "discovering" and planting his nation's flag on new worlds, because he called for a U.S. colony on the moon early in the next century. And forecast a mission to Mars in the year 2019.

The "patriotism" that Chauncey Depew invoked in celebrating Columbus was profoundly tied to the notion of the inferiority of the conquered peoples. Columbus' attacks on the Indians were justified by their status as sub-humans. The taking of Texas and much of Mexico by the United States just before the Civil War was done with the same racist rationale. Sam Houston, the first governor of Texas, proclaimed: "The Anglo-Saxon race must pervade the whole southern extremity of this vast continent. The Mexicans are no better than the Indians and I see no reason why we should not take their land."

At the start of the twentieth century, the violence of the new American expansionism into the Caribbean and the Pacific was accepted because we were dealing with lesser beings.

In the year 1900, Chauncey DePew, now a U.S. Senator, spoke again in Carnegie Hall, this time to support Theodore Roosevelt's candidacy for vice-president. Celebrating the conquest of the Philippines as a beginning of the American penetration of China and more, he proclaimed:

> The guns of Dewey in Manila Bay were heard across Asia and Africa, they echoed through the palace at Peking and brought to the Oriental mind a new and potent force among western nations. We, in common with the countries of Europe, are striving to enter the limitless markets of the east.... These people respect nothing but power. I believe the Philippines will be enormous markets and sources of wealth.

Theodore Roosevelt, who appears endlessly on lists of our "great presidents," and whose face is one of the four colossal sculptures of American presidents (along with Washington, Jefferson, Lincoln) carved into Mount Rushmore in South Dakota, was the quintessential racist-imperialist. He was furious, back in 1893, when President Cleveland failed to annex Hawaii, telling the Naval War College it was "a crime against white civilization." In his book *The Strenuous Life*, Roosevelt wrote:

> Of course our whole national history has been one of expansion...that the barbarians recede or are conquered...is due solely to the power of the mighty civilized races which have not lost the fighting instinct.

An Army officer in the Philippines put it even more bluntly: "There is no use mincing words.... We exterminated the American Indians and I guess most of us are proud of it...and we must have no scruples about exterminating this other race standing in the way of progress and enlightenment, if it is necessary..."

The official historian of the Indies in the early sixteenth century, Fernandez de Oviedo, did not deny what was done to natives by the *conquistadores*. He described "innumerable cruel deaths as countless as the stars." But this was acceptable, because "to use gunpowder against pagans is to offer incense to the Lord."

(One is reminded of President McKinley's decision to send the army and navy to take the Philippines, saying it was the duty of the United States to "Christianize and civilize" the Filipinos.)

Against Las Casas' pleas for mercy to the Indians, the theologian Juan Gines de Sepulveda declared: "How can we doubt that these people, so uncivilized, so barbaric, so contaminated with so many sins and obscenities, have been justly conquered."

Sepulveda in the year 1531 visited his former college in Spain and was outraged by seeing the students there protesting Spain's war against Turkey. The students were saying: "All war...is contrary to the Catholic religion."

This led him to write a philosophical defense of the Spanish treatment of the Indians. He quoted Aristotle, who wrote in his *Politics* that some people were "slaves by nature," who "should be hunted down like wild beasts in order to bring them to the correct way of life."

Las Casas responded: "Let us send Aristotle packing, for we have in our favor the command of Christ: Thou shalt love thy neighbor as thyself."

The dehumanization of the "enemy" has been a necessary accompaniment to wars of conquest. It is easier to explain atrocities if they are committed against infidels, or people of an inferior race. Slavery and racial segregation in the United States, and European imperialism in Asia and Africa, were justified in this way.

The bombing of Vietnamese villages by the United States, the search and destroy missions, the My Lai massacre, were all made palatable to their perpetrators by the idea that the victims were not human. They were "gooks" or "Communists," and deserved what they received.

In the Gulf War, the dehumanization of the Iraqis consisted of not recognizing their existence. We were not bombing women, children, not bombing and shelling ordinary Iraqi young men in the act of flight and surrender. We were acting against a Hitler-like monster, Saddam Hussein, although the people we were killing were the Iraqi victims of this monster. When General Colin Powell was asked about Iraqi casualties he said that was "really not a matter I am terribly interested in."

The American people were led to accept the violence of the war in Iraq because the Iraqis were made invisible—because the United States only used "smart bombs." The major media ignored the enormous death toll in Iraq, ignored the report of the Harvard medical team that visited Iraq shortly after the war and found that tens of thousands of Iraqi children were dying because of the bombing of the water supply and the resultant epidemics of disease.

The celebrations of Columbus are declared to be celebrations not just of his maritime exploits but of "progress," of his arrival in the Bahamas as the beginning of that much-praised five hundred years of "Western civilization." But those concepts need to be re-examined. When Gandhi was once asked what he thought about Western civilization, he replied: "It's a good idea."

The point is not to deny the benefits of "progress" and "civilization"—advances in technology, knowledge, science, health, education, and standards of living. But there is a question to be asked: progress yes, but at what human cost?

Is progress simply to be measured in the statistics of industrial and technological change, without regard to the consequences of that "progress" for human beings? Would we accept a Russian justification of Stalin's rule, including the enormous toll in human suffering, on the ground that he made Russia a great industrial power?

I recall that in my high school classes in American history when we came to the period after the Civil War, roughly the years between that War and World War I, it was looked on as the Gilded Age, the period of the great Industrial Revolution, when the United States became an economic giant. I remember how thrilled we were to learn of the dramatic growth of the steel and oil industries, of the building of the great fortunes, of the criss-crossing of the country by the railroads.

We were not told of the human cost of this great industrial progress: how the huge production of cotton came from the labor of black slaves; how the textile industry was built up by the labor of young girls who went into the mills at twelve and died at twenty-five; how the railroads were constructed by Irish and Chinese immigrants who were literally worked to death, in the heat of summer and cold of winter; how working people, immigrants and native-born, had to go out on strike and be beaten by police and jailed by National Guardsmen before they could win the eight-hour day; how the children of the working-class, in the slums of the city, had to drink polluted water, and how they died early of malnutrition and disease. All this in the name of "progress."

And yes, there are huge benefits from industrialization, science, technology, medicine. But so far, in these five hundred years of Western civilization, of Western domination of the rest of the world, most of those benefits have gone to a small part of the human race. For billions of people in the Third World, they still face starvation, homelessness, disease, the early deaths of their children.

Did the Columbus expeditions mark the transition from savagery to civilization? What of the Indian civilizations which had been built up over thousands of years before Columbus came? Las Casas and others marveled at the spirit of sharing and generosity which marked the Indian societies, the communal buildings in which they lived, their aesthetic sensibilities, the egalitarianism among men and women.

The British colonists in North America were startled at the democracy of the Iroquois—the tribes who occupied much of New

York and Pennsylvania. The American historian Gary Nash describes Iroquois culture: "No laws and ordinances, sheriffs and constables, judges and juries, or courts or jails—the apparatus of authority in European societies—were to be found in the northeast woodlands prior to European arrival. Yet boundaries of acceptable behavior were firmly set. Though priding themselves on the autonomous individual, the Iroquois maintained a strict sense of right and wrong..."

In the course of westward expansion, the new nation, the United States, stole the Indians' land, killed them when they resisted, destroyed their sources of food and shelter, pushed them into smaller and smaller sections of the country, went about the systematic destruction of Indian society. At the time of the Black Hawk War in the 1830s—one of hundreds of wars waged against the Indians of North America—Lewis Cass, the governor of the Michigan territory, referred to his taking of millions of acres from the Indians as "the progress of civilization." He said: "A barbarous people cannot live in contact with a civilized community."

We get a sense of how "barbarous" these Indians were when, in the 1880s, Congress prepared legislation to break up the communal lands in which Indians still lived, into small private possessions, what today some people would call, admiringly, "privatization." Senator Henry Dawes, author of this legislation, visited the Cherokee Nation, and described what he found: "...there was not a family in that whole nation that had not a home of its own. There was not a pauper in that nation, and the nation did not owe a dollar...it built its own schools and its hospitals. Yet the defect of the system was apparent. They have got as far as they can go, because they own their land in common...there is not enterprise to make your home any better than that of your neighbors. There is no selfishness, which is at the bottom of civilization."

That selfishness at the bottom of "civilization" is connected with what drove Columbus on, and what is much-praised today, as American political leaders and the media speak about how the West will do a great favor to the Soviet Union and Eastern Europe by introducing "the profit motive."

Granted, there may be certain ways in which the incentive of profit may be helpful in economic development, but that incentive, in the history of the "free market" in the West, has had horrendous consequences. It led, throughout the centuries of "Western Civilization," to a ruthless imperialism.

In Joseph Conrad's novel *Heart of Darkness*, written in the 1890s, after some time spent in the Upper Congo of Africa, he describes the work done by black men in chains on behalf of white men who were interested only in ivory. He writes: "The word 'ivory' rang in the air, was whispered, was sighed. You would think they were praying to it.... To tear treasure out of the bowels of the land was their desire, with no more moral purpose at the back of it than there is in burglars breaking into a safe."

The uncontrolled drive for profit has led to enormous human suffering, exploitation, slavery, cruelty in the workplace, dangerous working conditions, child labor, the destruction of land and forests, the poisoning of the air we breathe, the water we drink, the food we eat.

In his 1933 autobiography, Chief Luther Standing Bear wrote: "True the white man brought great change. But the varied fruits of his civilization, though highly colored and inviting, are sickening and deadening. And if it be the part of civilization to maim, rob, and thwart, then what is progress? I am going to venture that the man who sat on the ground in his tipi meditating on life and its meaning, accepting the kinship of all creatures, and acknowledging unity with the universe of things, was infusing into his being the true essence of civilization."

The present threats to the environment have caused a reconsideration among scientists and other scholars of the value of "progress" as it has been so far defined. In December of 1991, there was a two-day conference at MIT, in which fifty scientists and historians discussed the idea of progress in Western thought. Here is part of the report on that conference in the *Boston Globe*.

"In a world where resources are being squandered and the environment poisoned, participants in an MIT conference said yesterday, it is time for people to start thinking in terms of sustainability and stability rather than growth and progress.... Verbal fireworks and heated exchanges that sometimes grew into shouting matches punctuated the discussions among scholars of economics, religion, medicine, history and the sciences."

One of the participants, historian Leo Marx, said that working toward a more harmonious co-existence with nature is itself a kind of progress, but different than the traditional one in which people try to overpower nature.

So, to look back at Columbus in a critical way is to raise all these questions about progress, civilization, our relations with one another, our relationship to the natural world.

You probably have heard—as I have, quite often—that it is wrong for us to treat the Columbus story the way we do. What they say is: "You are taking Columbus out of context, looking at him with the eyes of the twentieth century. You must not superimpose the values of our time on events that took place 500 years ago. That is ahistorical."

I find this argument strange. Does it mean that cruelty, exploitation, greed, enslavement, violence against helpless people, are values peculiar to the fifteenth and sixteenth centuries? And that we in the twentieth century, are beyond that? Are there not certain human values which are common to the age of Columbus and to our own? Proof of that is that both in his time and in ours there were enslavers and exploiters; in both his time and ours there were those who protested against that, on behalf of human rights.

It is encouraging that, in this year of the quincentennial, there is a wave of protest, unprecedented in all the years of celebration of Columbus, all over the United States, and throughout the Americas. Much of this protest is being led by Indians, who are organizing conferences and meetings, who are engaging in acts of civil disobedience, who are trying to educate the American public about what really happened five hundred years ago, and what it tells us about the issues of our time.

There is a new generation of teachers in our schools, and many of them are insisting that the Columbus story be told from the point of view of the native Americans. In the fall of 1990 I was telephoned from Los Angeles by a talk-show host who wanted to discuss Columbus. Also on the line was a high school student in that city, named Blake Lindsey, who had insisted on addressing the Los Angeles City Council to oppose the traditional Columbus Day celebration. She told them of the genocide committed by the Spaniards against the Arawak Indians. The City council did not respond.

Someone called in on that talk show, introducing herself as a woman who had emigrated from Haiti. She said: "The girl is right— we have no Indians left—in our last uprising against the government the people knocked down the statue of Columbus and now it is in the basement of the city hall in Port-au-Prince." The caller finished by saying: "Why don't we build statues for the aborigines?"

Despite the textbooks still in use, more teachers are questioning, more students are questioning. Bill Bigelow reports on the reactions of his students after he introduces them to reading material which contradicts the traditional histories. One student wrote: "In 1492, Columbus sailed the ocean blue.... That story is about as complete as Swiss cheese."

Another wrote a critique of her American history textbook to the publisher, Allyn and Bacon, pointing to many important omissions in that text. She said: "I'll just pick one topic to keep it simple. How about Columbus?"

Another student: "It seemed to me as if the publishers had just printed up some glory story that was supposed to make us feel more patriotic about our country.... They want us to look at our country as great and powerful and forever right.... We're being fed lies."

When students discover that in the very first history they learn—the story of Columbus—they have not been told the whole truth, it leads to a healthy skepticism about all of their historical education. One of Bigelow's students, named Rebecca, wrote: "What does it matter who discovered America, really?... But the thought that I've been lied to all my life about this, and who knows what else, really makes me angry."

This new critical thinking in the schools and in the colleges seems to frighten those who have glorified what is called "Western civilization." Reagan's Secretary of Education, William Bennett, in his 1984 "Report on the Humanities in Higher Education," writes of Western civilization as "our common culture...its highest ideas and aspirations."

One of the most ferocious defenders of Western civilization is philosopher Allan Bloom, who wrote *The Closing of the American Mind* in a spirit of panic at what the social movements of the Sixties had done to change the educational atmosphere of American universities. He was frightened by the student demonstrations he saw at Cornell, which he saw as a terrible interference with education.

Bloom's idea of education was a small group of very smart students, in an elite university, studying Plato and Aristotle, and refusing to be disturbed in their contemplation by the noise outside their windows of students rallying against racism or protesting against the war in Vietnam.

As I read him, I was reminded of some of my colleagues, when I was teaching in a black college in Atlanta, Georgia at the time of the civil rights movement, who shook their heads in disapproval when our students left their classes to sit-in, to be arrested, in protest against racial segregation. These students were neglecting their education, they said. In fact, these students were learning more in a few weeks of participation in social struggle than they could learn in a year of going to class.

What a narrow, stunted understanding of education! It corresponds perfectly to the view of history which insists that Western civilization is the summit of human achievement. As Bloom wrote in his book: "...only in the Western nations, i.e. those influenced by Greek philosophy, is there some willingness to doubt the identification of the good with one's own way." Well, if this willingness to doubt is the hallmark of Greek philosophy, then Bloom and his fellow idolizers of Western civilization are ignorant of that philosophy.

If Western civilization is considered the high point of human progress, the United States is the best representative of this civilization. Here is Allan Bloom again: "This is the American moment in world history.... America tells one story: the unbroken, ineluctable progress of freedom and equality. From its first settlers and its political foundings on, there has been no dispute that freedom and equality are the essence of justice for us..."

Yes, tell black people and native Americans and the homeless and those without health insurance, and all the victims abroad of American foreign policy that America "tells one story...freedom and equality."

Western civilization is complex. It represents many things, some decent, some horrifying. We would have to pause before celebrating it uncritically when we note that David Duke, the Louisiana Ku Klux Klan member and ex-Nazi says that people have got him wrong. "The common strain in my thinking," he told a reporter, "is my love for Western civilization."

We who insist on looking critically at the Columbus story, and indeed at everything in our traditional histories, are often accused of insisting on Political Correctness, to the detriment of free speech. I find this odd. It is the guardians of the old stories, the orthodox histories, who refuse to widen the spectrum of ideas, to take in new books, new approaches, new information, new views of history. They, who claim to believe in "free markets" do not believe in a free marketplace of ideas, any more than they believe in a free marketplace of goods and services. In both material goods and in ideas, they want the market dominated by those who have always held power and wealth. They worry that if new ideas enter the marketplace, people may begin to rethink the social arrangements that have given us so much suffering, so much violence, so much war these last five hundred years of "civilization."

Of course we had all that before Columbus arrived in this hemisphere, but resources were puny, people were isolated from one another, and the possibilities were narrow. In recent centuries, however, the world has become amazingly small, our possibilities for creating a decent society have enormously magnified, and so the excuses for hunger, ignorance, violence, racism, no longer exist.

In rethinking our history, we are not just looking at the past, but at the present, and trying to look at it from the point of view of those who have been left out of the benefits of so-called civilization. It is a simple but profoundly important thing we are trying to accomplish, to look at the world from other points of view. We need to do that, as we come into the next century, if we want this coming century to be different, if we want it to be, not an American century, or a Western century, or a white century, or a male century, or any nation's, any group's century, but a century for the human race.

15

How Free is
Higher Education?

I was invited in 1991 to write this essay as part of a symposium on the university for the *Gannett Center Journal*, which came out of Columbia University. There had been going on for some time a hot national debate on "multi-culturalism," on freedom of speech in the university, on "political correctness." As a result of the movements of the Sixties, changes had taken place in American education, and some of these changes were causing a kind of hysteria among conservatives. I thought I would add my bit to the debate, based on my own experience in higher education.

E ducation has always inspired fear among those who want to keep the existing distributions of power and wealth as they are.

In my thirty years of teaching—in a small southern college, in a large northeastern university—I have often observed that fear. And I think I understand what it is based on. The educational environment is unique in our society: It is the only situation where an adult, looked up to as a mentor, is alone with a group of young people for a protracted and officially sanctioned period of time and can assign whatever reading he or she chooses, and discuss with these young people any subject under the sun. The subject may be defined by the curriculum, by the catalog course description, but this is a minor impediment to a bold and imaginative teacher, especially in literature, philosophy and the social sciences, where there are unlimited possibilities for free discussion of social and political issues.

That would seem to be an educational ideal, an arena for free discussion, assuming a diversity of viewpoints from a variety of teachers, of the most important issues of our time. Yet it is precisely that situation, in the classrooms of higher education, which frightens the guardians of the status quo.

They declare their admiration for such freedom in principle, and suggest that radicals are insufficiently grateful for its existence. But when teachers actually *use* this freedom, introducing new subjects, new readings, outrageous ideas, challenging authority, criticizing "Western civilization," amending the "canon" of great books as listed by certain educational authorities of the past, then the self-appointed guardians of "high culture" become enraged.

Early in my teaching career I decided that I would make the most of the special freedom that is possible in a classroom. I would introduce what I felt to be the most important, and therefore the most controversial, questions in my class.

When I was assigned, as a young professor at Spelman College, a college for black women in Atlanta, a course in "Constitutional Law," I changed the course title to "Civil Liberties" and departed from the canonized recital of Supreme Court cases. I did not ignore the most important of these cases, but I also talked with the students about social movements for justice and asked what role these movements played in changing the environment within which Supreme Court decisions were made.

When I taught American history, I ignored the canon of the traditional textbook, in which the heroic figures were mostly presidents, generals and industrialists. In those texts, wars were treated as problems in military strategy and not in morality; Christopher Columbus and Andrew Jackson and Theodore Roosevelt were treated as heroes in the march of democracy, with not a word from the objects of their violence.

I suggested that we approach Columbus and Jackson from the perspective of their victims, that we look at the magnificent feat of the transcontinental railroad from the viewpoint of the Irish and Chinese laborers who, in building it, died by the thousands.

Was I committing that terrible sin which is arousing the anger of today's fundamentalists: "politicizing the curriculum"? Is there any rendition of constitutional law, any recounting of American history that can escape being *political*—that is, expressing a political point of view? To treat Theodore Roosevelt as a hero (which is usually not done overtly, but in an expression of quiet admiration)—is that less "political" than pointing to his role as an early imperialist, a forerunner of a long string of crude U.S. interventions in the Caribbean?

I have no doubt that I was taking a political stand when, in the early 1960s, I expressed respect for my students who missed classes to demonstrate in downtown Atlanta against racial segregation. In doing that, was I being more political than the fundamentalist Allan Bloom, at Cornell, who pointed with pride to the fact that the students in his seminar on Plato and Aristotle stuck to their studies and refused to participate in the social conflict outside the seminar room?

In my teaching I never concealed my political views: my detestation of war and militarism, my anger at radial inequality, my belief in a democratic socialism, in a rational and just distribution of world's wealth. To pretend to an "objectivity" that was neither possible nor desirable seemed to me dishonest.

I made it clear to my students at the start of each course that they would be getting *my* point of view on the subjects under discussion, that I would try to be fair to other points of view, that I would scrupulously uphold their right to disagree with me.

My students had a long experience of political indoctrination before they arrived in my class—in the family, in high school, in movies and television. They would hear viewpoints other than mine in other courses, and for the rest of their lives. I insisted on my right to enter my opinions in the marketplace of ideas, so long dominated by orthodoxy.

Surely the expression of "political views" (what is just, or unjust? what can citizens do?) is inevitable in education. It may be done overtly, honestly, or it may be there subtly. But it is always there, however the textbook, by its very bulk and dullness, pretends to neutrality, however noncommittal is the teacher.

It is inevitably there because all education involves *selection*—of events, of voices, of books—and any insistence on one list of great books or great figures or great events is a partial (in both senses of that term) rendering of our cultural heritage.

Therefore it seems to me that the existence of free expression in higher education must mean the opportunity for many points of view, many political biases, to be presented to students. This requires a true pluralism of readings, ideas, viewpoints—a genuinely free marketplace of thought and culture. Let both Shakespeare and Wole Soyinka, Bach and Leonard Bernstein, Dickens and W.E.B. Du Bois, John Stuart Mill and Zora Neale Hurston, Rembrandt and Picasso, Plato and Laotzu, Locke and Marx, Aeschylus and August Wilson, Jane Austen and Gabriel Garcia Márquez be available to students.

Such a free marketplace of ideas does not depend essentially on "the curriculum." How many words have been wasted moving those empty shells around the debating table! What is crucial is the content of those shells, which depends on who the teachers are and who the students are. A thoughtful teacher can take a course labeled "Western Civilization" and enlarge its content with an exciting global perspective. Another teacher can be given a course grandly called "World Civilization" and give the student an eclectic, limp recounting of dull events and meaningless dates.

That pluralism in thought that is required for truly free expression in higher education has never been realized. Its crucial elements—an ideologically diverse faculty, a heterogeneous student body (in class, race, sex—words that bring moans from the keepers of the "higher culture")—have always been under attack from outside and from inside the colleges and universities.

McCarthyism, in which the corporate nature of academic institutions revealed itself in the surrender of university administrators to government inquisitors (see Ellen Schrecker's book *No Ivory Tower: McCarthyism in the Universities* for the details), was only the most flagrant of the attacks on freedom of expression. More subtle, more persistent, has been the control of faculty appointments, contract renewals and tenure (inevitably with political considerations) by colleagues, but especially by administrators, who are the universities' links with the dominant forces of American society—the government, the corporations, the military.

Boston University, where I taught for many years, is not too far from typical, with its panoply of military and government connections—ROTC chapters for every military service, former government officials given special faculty posts, the board of trustees dominated by corporate executives, a president eager to curry favor with powerful politicos. Almost all colleges and universities are organized as administrative hierarchies in which a president and trustees, usually well connected to wealthy and important people in the outside world, make the critical decisions as to who may enjoy the freedom of the classroom to speak to the young people of the new generation.

Higher education, while enjoying some special privileges, is still part of the American system, which is an ingenious, sophisticated system of control. It is not totalitarian; what permits it to be called a democracy is that it allows apertures of liberty on the supposition that this will not endanger the basic contours of wealth and power in the society. It trusts that the very flexibility of a partially free system will assure its survival, even contribute to its strength.

Our government is so confident of its power that it can risk allowing some political choice to the people, who can vote for Democrats or Republicans but find huge obstacles of money and bureaucracy if they want an alternative. Our corporations are so wealthy that they can afford some distribution of wealth to a supportive middle class, but not to the 30 or 40 million people who live in the cellars of society.

The system can allow special space for free expression in its cultural institutions: the theater, the arts, the media. But the size of that space is controlled by money and power; the profit motive limits what is put on stage or screen; government officials dominate the informational role of the news media.

Yes, there is, indeed, a special freedom of expression in the academy. How can I at Boston University, or Noam Chomsky at MIT, or David Montgomery at Yale, deny that we have had more freedom in the university than we would have in business or other professions? But those who tolerate us know that our numbers are few, that our students, however excited by new ideas, go out into a world of economic pressures and exhortations to caution. And they know too that they can point to us as an example of the academy's openness to all ideas.

True, there is a tradition of academic freedom, but it is based on a peculiar unspoken contract. The student, in return for the economic security of a career and several years with some degree of free intellectual play, is expected upon graduation to become an obedient citizen, participating happily in the nation's limited pluralism (be a Republican or a Democrat, but please, nothing else).

The boundaries for free expression in the university, though broader than in the larger society, are still watched carefully. When that freedom is used, even by a small minority, to support social change considered dangerous by the guardians of the *status quo*, the alarm goes out: "The Communists are infiltrating our institutions"; "Marxists have taken over the curriculum"; "feminists and black militants are destroying classical education."

Their reaction approaches hysteria: "With a few notable exceptions, our most prestigious liberal arts colleges and universities have installed the entire radical menu at the center of their humanities curriculum," says Roger Kimball in his book *Tenured Radicals*. The shrillness of such alarms is never proportionate to the size of the radical threat. But the Establishment takes no chances. Thus J. Edgar Hoover and Joseph McCarthy saw imminent danger of communist control of the U.S. government; protectors of "the canon" see "tenured radicals" taking over higher education. The axes then get sharpened.

Yes, some of us radicals have somehow managed to get tenure. But far from dominating higher education, we remain a carefully watched minority. Some of us may continue to speak and write and teach as we like, but we have seen the axe fall countless times on colleagues less lucky. And who can deny the chilling effect this has had on other faculty, with or without tenure, who have censored themselves rather than risk a loss of promotion, a lower salary, a nonrenewal of contract, a denial of tenure?

Perhaps, after all, Boston University cannot be considered typical, having had for 20 years probably the most authoritarian, the most politically watchful university president in the country. But although it is hard to match John Silber as an educational tyrant, he can be considered (I base this on spending some time at other universities) not a departure from the norm, but an exaggeration of it.

Have we had freedom of expression at Boston University?

A handful of radical teachers, in a faculty of over a thousand, was enough to have John Silber go into fits over our presence on campus, just as certain observers of higher education are now getting apoplectic over what they see as radical dominance nationwide. These are ludicrous fantasies, but they lead to attacks on the freedom of expression of those faculty who manage to overcome that prudent self-control so prominent among academics. At Boston it must have been such fantasies that led Silber to determinedly destroy the faculty union, which was a minor threat to his control over faculty. He handled appointments and tenure with the very political criteria that his conservative educational companions so loudly decry. In at least seven cases that I know of, where the candidates were politically undesirable by Silber's standards, he ignored overwhelming faculty recommendations and refused them tenure.

Did I have freedom of expression in my classroom? I did, because I followed Aldous Huxley's advice: "Liberties are not given; they are taken." But it was obviously infuriating to John Silber that every semester 400 students signed up to take my courses, whether it was "Law and Justice in America" or "An Introduction to Political Theory." And so he did what is often done in the academy; he engaged in petty harassments—withholding salary raises, denying teaching assistants. He also threatened to fire me (and four other members of the union) when we held our classes on the street rather than cross the picket lines of striking secretaries.

The fundamentalists of politics—the Reagans and Bushes and Helmses—want to pull the strings of control tighter on the distribution of wealth and power and civil liberties. The fundamentalists of law, the Borks and Rehnquists, want to interpret the Constitution so as to put strict limits on the legal possibilities for social reform. The fundamentalists of education fear the possibilities inherent in the unique freedom of discussion that we find in higher education.

And so, under the guise of defending "the common culture" or "disinterested scholarship" or "Western civilization," they attack that freedom. They fear exactly what some of us hope for, that if students are given wider political choices in the classroom than they get in the polling booth or the workplace, they may become social rebels. They may join movements for racial or sexual equality, or against war, or, even more dangerous, work for what James Madison feared as he argued for a conservative Constitution: "an equal division of property." Let us hope so.

16

"A University Should Not Be a Democracy"

When I first began teaching, I had a rather naïve idea that colleges and universities, however the world outside was dominated by money and power, were special havens for freedom of expression and democracy. It did not take long for me to be disabused of that idea. My first personal experience was at Spelman College in Atlanta, where my political activism offended the college president and—though I was a full professor, with tenure, and chair of the history department, presumably secure—he fired me, with forty-eight hours notice, for "insubordination," a charge which was undoubtedly true. The university, as in the title of Ellen Schrecker's book on McCarthyism in higher education, is "No Ivory Tower," but a battleground in which students, faculty, university workers have to struggle constantly for democratic rights. Boston University was a particularly intense site in that struggle. In this essay, I tried to put what happened there, under the presidency of John Silber, in the larger context of the attempt of the national establishment, after the exuberant democracy of the Sixties, to restore order and authority. This appeared in *The Progressive*, June 1980, under the title "A Showcase of Repression."

Think a bit about the history of these past twenty-five years in the United States—the years of the black revolt and the movements of women, prisoners, native Americans; the years of the great campaign against the Indochina war and the illumination of Watergate. It was in these twenty-five years that the Establishment began to lose control of the minds, the loyalties of the American people. And since about 1975, the Establishment has been working steadily, with some desperation, to reassert that control.

In those years of the movements, great numbers of Americans began to take democracy seriously, to think for themselves, to doubt the experts, to distrust the political leaders, and to lose faith in the military, the corporations, even the once-untouchable FBI and CIA. In mid-1975, the Harris poll, looking at the years since 1966, reported that public confidence in the military had dropped from 62 percent to 29 percent, in business from 55 percent to 18 percent, in the President and Congress from 42 percent to 13 percent. When the Survey Research Center of the University of Michigan posed the question, "Is the Government run by a few big interests looking out for themselves?" the answer in 1964 was "yes" from 53 percent of those polled.

Harvard political scientist Samuel Huntington reported to the Trilateral Commission—a group of Establishment intellectuals and political leaders from the United States, Europe, and Japan, assembled by David Rockefeller and Zbigniew Brzezinski in the early 1970s—on what he called "The Democratic Distemper." "The 1960s witnessed a dramatic upsurge of democratic fervor in America," Huntington observed, and that troubled him. He noted that in 1960 only 18 percent of the public believed the Government was spending too much on defense, but by 1969 this figure had jumped to 52 percent. He wrote:

> "The essence of the democratic surge of the 1960s was a general challenge to existing systems of authority, public and private. In one form or another, this challenge manifested itself in the family, the university, business, public and private associations, politics, the governmental bureaucracy, and the military services. People no longer felt the same obligation to obey those whom they had previously considered superior to themselves in age, rank, status, expertise, character, or talents."

Huntington was worried: "The question necessarily arises, however, whether if a new threat to security should materialize in the future (as it inevitably will at some point), the Government will possess the authority to command the resources, as well as the sacrifices, which are necessary to meet that threat." We were beset, he wrote, by "an excess of democracy." He suggested "desirable limits to the extension of political democracy."

Let us imagine the nation's elite addressing itself to the problem posed by Huntington. If the proper respect for authority is to be regained, then surely the universities must do their job. It has usually been possible to count on them to fill the lower ranks of the Establishment with technical and professional people who, fairly well paid and engrossed in their own advancement, would serve as loyal guards for the system. But in the early 1960s, young black rebels came off the college campuses and formed the militant cutting edge of the black movement, and then the universities became the focal points of teach-ins and demonstrations against the war.

True, the loss of allegiance extended far beyond the campus, into the workplaces and homes of ordinary Americans, into the Army ranks where working-class GIs turned against the war. Still, with twelve million young people in college, the fear of a working-class-professional-class coalition for social change makes it especially important to educate for obedience. And the intensifying economic pressures of unemployment and inflation may suggest to the national elite that it is now easier, and also more necessary, to teach the teachers as well as the students the advisability of submitting to higher authority.

Thus, it may be part of some larger reordering of the nation's mind when the president of Boston University, John Silber, says on national television (CBS's *60 Minutes*, viewed by thirty million), "A university should not be a democracy.... The more democratic a university is, the lousier it is."

As soon as Silber became B.U.'s president in 1971, he began to act out his philosophy by destroying what is at the heart of humanistic education: the idea that students and faculty should have a decisive voice about the way education takes place. And he had an additional target: the idea that workers at the university should have some right to decide the conditions of their work.

Those of us who are involved in the intense, sometimes bizarre battles at Boston University have not had much time to step back and look for some grand national design into which we might fit. Furthermore, it seems immodest; we have not yet become accustomed to the fact that our campus, with its nondescript assortment of buildings straddling Commonwealth Avenue in the heart of the city, with its heterogeneous enrollment of 20,000 students, has begun to attract the attention of the country. It is as if a rare disease had broken out somewhere, and was being observed by everyone with much curiosity and a bit of apprehension.

John Silber, formerly a professor of philosophy at the University of Texas, had hardly settled into the presidential mansion—a twenty-room house, rent-free, only one of the many fringe benefits adding up to perhaps $100,000 a year which augment his $100,000 salary—

when he embarked on the process the Germans call *Gleichschaltung:* "straightening things out." He quickly made it clear that he would not tolerate student interference with military recruiting at B.U. for the war in Vietnam. Early in 1972, his administration invited Marine recruiters to a campus building. When students sat down on the steps of that building, remaining there firmly but peaceably, he called the police. Arrests and beatings followed, and Silber said he was maintaining "an open university."

The university that was "open" to the Marine Corps turned out to be closed to the campus chapter of Students for a Democratic Society (SDS), which lost its charter and its right to meet on campus because a scuffle had taken place during an SDS demonstration. The logic was established: SDS was a violent organization, while the Marine Corps had a well-known record for pacifism.

A series of demonstrations followed, to which police were called again and again, and which they broke up with arrests and brutal beatings. The turmoil led to a huge assembly of the Faculty Senate, which voted overwhelmingly that Marine recruiting should be halted until faculty and students could discuss and vote on whether it should be resumed. Silber simply ignored the resolution. That summer, without the called-for campus discussion, he polled the faculty through the mail, not specifically asking about Marine recruiting, but rather about whether the faculty wanted an "open university." The answer, of course, was yes, and the recruiters were on campus to stay.

That fall, the students did vote, in an unprecedented turnout. A large majority rejected the policy of military recruiting on campus. Silber ignored them, too. Picketing students, he said, were "primates," and votes did not matter. "I would be much more impressed," he told the student newspaper, the *Daily Free Press*, "by a thoughtful document that was brought in by one single student than I would by a mindless referendum of 16,000." He would decide who was "thoughtful" and who was "mindless."

The centralization of power in Silber's hands, his contempt for faculty as well as students, his attempts to push tenured professors at the School of Theology into resigning, his repeated attacks on the tenure system—all this led to a burst of faculty unionization under the auspices of the American Association of University Professors (AAUP). Silber, confident of his oratorical powers, went to faculty meetings at the various colleges, arguing that a vote for unionization would mean the end of the "collegial" model and the introduction of the "industrial" model at Boston University. Nonetheless, the faculty voted by a clear majority for a union. In the next four years, the Silber administration spent huge sums of money before the National Labor Relations Board (NLRB) and in the courts, trying unsuccessfully to overturn that vote.

Silber's argument against the AAUP was that well-paid and articulate college professors don't need a union. But when other employees tried to act in concert to improve their situation, his administration did its best to beat them down. Workers at the Student Health Clinic were fired when they met to voice grievances. The NLRB, after lengthy hearings, ruled that the B.U. administration was guilty of unfair labor practices in firing seven employees and intimidating the rest.

In the spring of 1976, departmental budget cuts led to anger on all sides. Later, it was learned that while Silber was jacking up student tuition and telling the faculty there was no money for raises, he was putting several million dollars a year into "reserves" and listing these set-aside funds as "expenses" so that the budget barely showed a surplus.

There were calls for Silber's dismissal from ten of the fifteen deans, from faculties at various colleges in the university, from virtually every student organization, and finally from a Faculty Senate meeting. A committee of trustees, making its five-year evaluation of Silber, voted 7-to-1 that his contract should not be renewed. But he worked furiously at lining up trustee votes, found powerful allies on the board, and persuaded them to keep him in the presidency.

As part of the campaign for control, Silber began to put the screws to campus newspapers that criticized him. Advertising was withdrawn from the *B.U. News* (which had been a pioneering critic of the Vietnam War under the editorship of Ray Mungo), causing it to close. A new student publication called *Exposure*, pitilessly anti-Silber (one of its headlines referred to him as: "Mediocre Philosopher, Expert Chiseler"), had its funds—allocated from student activities fees—cut off. A new policy was adopted: Campus newspapers that wanted funding from student activities fees must submit to prior review of their copy by faculty advisers. Programs at the campus radio station, WBUR, came under scrutiny of Silber's administrators, and one news director was fired when he refused to censor the tape of a speech by William Kunstler which contained a joke about John Silber.

It also became more and more clear that any faculty member who spoke out against Silber was in danger of being denied tenure or, if tenured, of being denied a pay raise. Again and again, departmental recommendations of raises for certain faculty who were outspoken critics of the Silber Administration were overruled. Early in Silber's administration, Professor Richard Newman, who had taught in the social sciences for nine years, resigned from the University, and told the *B.U. News* that budget cuts had eliminated almost half the faculty of his department, including "three or four of the best young teacher-scholars in the country." Newman said, "To disagree with the President is to be put on the Enemies List."

Students, faculty, and staff fought back. The *B.U. Exposure* raised outside money to keep publishing its stories of administration shenanigans. There was evidence that Silber was pushing law school applicants to the top of the list when financial contributions from their families were sought. "I am not ashamed to sell these indulgences," he told a meeting of the trustees, and somehow the *Exposure* got hold of the transcript. It was a joke, Silber explained. And later, when the *Exposure* reprinted an administration memorandum in which a wealthy trustee was described as having sought and received "pre-admission" to the law school for his two small grandchildren "for the twenty-first century," Silber said that was a joke, too—lots of jokes from an administration known for its utter lack of humor.

Clerical workers on campus, underpaid and harassed, began organizing a union and won an NLRB election. Librarians formed a union and won their election. The Silber administration refused to negotiate with them, as it had with the faculty union. When the buildings-and-grounds workers, long unionized, went on strike for a week in the fall of 1978, members of the other unions, along with students, formed large picket lines and held support rallies. They were getting ready for a big labor upsurge the following spring.

In April 1979, Boston University, whose employees were now probably the most organized of any private university in the country, became the most strike-ridden in the country. The administration, having exhausted its court appeals, had to enter into negotiations with the faculty union. It came to an agreement, under the faculty threat of an April strike deadline, then reneged on the agreement at the last moment.

The faculty called a strike that same evening. The next morning, the lines were up at twenty-one buildings. By noon, hundreds of picketing faculty were joined by clerical workers and librarians insisting that the administration negotiate with them on their own demands.

The Silber administration had not expected such a reaction. The strike quickly crippled the operations of the university. Of 800 faculty in the bargaining unit, at least 700 were observing the picket lines, and of these about 350 were picketing. It was a rare, perhaps unique event in the history of American higher education—professors and secretaries walking the picket lines together in a common strike.

After nine days, the administration and faculty agreed on a contract providing substantial wage increases and a grievance procedure, but leaving most decisions on tenure and other matters still in the hands of the president and trustees. The clerical workers and librarians were still on the picket lines. With varying degrees of anguish, most of the faculty, feeling bound by a no-sympathy-strike clause in the contact, went back to work, but about seventy refused to cross the picket lines and held their classes out of doors or off campus. In nine more days, with the clerical workers and librarians holding firm, the administration agreed to negotiate, and everyone went back to work.

However, by late summer, the bargaining between the clerical workers and the administration broke down. Faculty and students returning for the fall semester found picket lines in place. It took a week for the strike to be settled by a contract agreement.

A small number of faculty had refused to cross the clerical workers' picket lines and either held their classes elsewhere or had colleagues take their classes. Five of us—political scientist Murray Levin, journalist Caryl Rivers, historian Fritz Ringer (president of the faculty union during the spring strike), psychologist Andrew Dibner, and I—were warned that we had violated the no-sympathy-strike provision. We replied that we had acted as individuals, according to our consciences, in expressing our support for the clerical workers. The Silber administration announced it was proceeding against us under the contract (we were all tenured professors) utilizing a provision for the suspension or dismissal of tenured professors on grounds of "gross neglect of duty or other just cause."

The charges against the B.U. Five, as we came to be known, lent new urgency to the work of the Committee to Save B.U., formed by faculty and students to rid the campus of the Silber machine.

Last December 18, a record number of faculty crowded into the largest auditorium on campus and listened to colleagues detail the charges against the Silber administration—mismanagement, centralization of decision-making, discrimination against women, violations of civil liberties, abusive and insulting behavior towards faculty.

Managers, whether of a government or of an institution, must learn how to gauge the capacity for rebellion so that they can head it off with the proper mix of repressions and concessions. The Silber administration had misjudged, when it reneged on the union contract in the spring of 1979, the faculty's willingness and readiness to strike. It misjudged again when it went after the B.U. Five. The threat to fire tenured faculty for honoring their convictions (Silber was quoted in the press as saying that faculty who signed union contacts had surrendered their right of conscience) aroused immediate protest.

Salvador Luria, Nobel Laureate in biology at MIT and a veteran of the antiwar movement, began circulating a petition among faculty at MIT, Harvard, and other colleges and universities in the Boston area, calling for the charges against the Five to be dropped and for Silber to be fired. Five hundred faculty in the Boston area signed the petition within two weeks. Another petition, signed by Luria, Noam Chomsky, historian John Womack of Harvard, and historian of science Everett Mendelsohn of Harvard, began circulating nationwide. The signatures came pouring in.

Alumni wrote letters to the B.U. trustees and the Boston newspapers. On campus, student groups called for the charges to be dropped and for Silber's removal.

The Massachusetts Community College Council, representing faculty at fifteen colleges, protested. A sociologist withdrew his request to be a visiting professor at B.U., citing the administration's action. The Massachusetts Sociological Association passed a resolution expressing its concern for "freedom of conscience." A visiting linguistics professor from Paris brought word back to France and a telegram came shortly after, signed by fifteen distinguished French academicians, declaring their support for the B.U. Five.

But the slick pro-Silber profile on *60 Minutes* drew letters of support from viewers around the country who saw Silber as the man who would make the dirty college kids clean up their rooms and whip the radical faculty into line.

This spring, Silber still seems to have a firm grasp on his Commonwealth Avenue fiefdom. The trustees have given no overt signs of disaffection. The faculty union is entangled in a hundred grievances in the slow machinery of the contract. B.U. students, just handed an outrageous 16 percent tuition increase, are only beginning to organize. The threat of punishment still keeps many faculty in line. Indeed, the Dean of the College of Liberal Arts has announced he is adding a new factor in determining merit raises: A faculty member's teaching performance and publications, however stellar, may be offset, he says, by "negative merit"—actions designed to "harm the University."

There are some signs, however, that the protests from all over the academic world are having an effect. In February, the administration, through the intercession of a committee appointed by the official Faculty Council, agreed to drop the charges against the B.U. Five, and to negotiate or arbitrate the question of punishment for faculty refusal to cross picket lines.

After six members of the Committee to Save B.U. appeared before the trustees, in an unprecedented contact with a board always remote from the faculty, it was learned that there were expressions of disaffection among the trustees, who have been Silber's last stronghold.

The board has welcomed Silber's enthusiasm for the banking and utilities interests they represent, as well as his friendliness toward the military. Silber has been a spokesman for nuclear power and against the evening out of utility rates to favor the small consumer. B.U. has an overseas program in which it services the American military with courses and degrees, and Silber has shown obvious deference to the Government's military needs in ROTC and recruiting.

Nevertheless, as faculty, secretaries, librarians, and buildings-and-grounds workers remain organized and determined to fight back, as students become increasingly resentful at being treated like peons in a banana republic, as protests from alumni and from the national academic community intensify, the trustees may have to reconsider. When risks become too great, the clubs of the Establishment sometimes decide to change to a form of control less crass and more conciliatory. To prevent more drastic upheaval, the board may replace Silber with its own version of a Gerald Ford or Jimmy Carter.

Back in 1976, John Silber wrote on the *op-ed* page of *The New York Times:*

> As Jefferson recognized, there is a natural aristocracy among men. The grounds of this are virtue and talent...Democracy freed from a counterfeit and ultimately destructive egalitarianism provides a society in which the wisest, the best, and the most dedicated assume positions of leadership.... As long as intelligence is better than stupidity, knowledge than ignorance, and virtue than vice, no university can be run except on an elitist basis.

That makes for a neat fit with the philosophy of Samuel Huntington and the Trilateral Commission as they react to the "excess of democracy" that sprang from the movements of the 1960s. The Establishment's need to reassert control over the universities expresses itself most blatantly in the authoritarianism of John Silber at Boston University, but there is some evidence of a national trend in higher education toward the punishment of dissent and toward more direct intervention by big business in the workings of the universities. Earlier this year, *The New York Times* reported that schools of business around the country—at Dartmouth, Duke, and Cornell, among others—now have "executives-in-residence," to match the more customary university practice of maintaining "artists-in-residence" and "writers-in-residence." And the American Council on Education has been urging colleges to recruit more aggressively and to increase their ties to business. Management and marketing consultants are now common presences on campuses, as are union-busting consultants and "security" advisers.

As the economic situation of the universities becomes more precarious and faculties shrink, it becomes easier to get rid of undesirables, whether political dissidents or just troublesome campus critics. If they are untenured, dismissal is a simple process. If they are tenured, some ingenuity is required. The files of the American Association of University Professors show, according to one member of the AAUP's committee on academic freedom, "a disturbing number of mean little cases this year." He said, "There seem to be many tenth-rate John Silbers around."

The AAUP refers to an increasing number of "indecencies." At Central Washington State University, a tenured professor of political science, Charles Stasny, was recently fired by the trustees for "insubordination" after he missed several classes because he attended a scholarly meeting in Israel. The administration had first approved his departure, then opposed it. At Nichols College, outside Worcester, Massachusetts, a non-tenured professor who questioned the leadership of the college president was summarily dismissed. At Philander Smith College in Little Rock, two tenured professors and one non-tenured faculty member were fired last June and told to leave the campus the same day; they had complained to student newspapers and the trustees about the lack of academic freedom on campus.

Whether at universities or an other workplaces, whether in the United States or in other countries, we seem to face the same challenge: The corporations and the military, shaken and frightened by the rebellious movements of recent decades, are trying to reassert their undisputed power. We have a responsibility not only to resist, but to build on the heritage of those movements, and to move toward the ideals of egalitarianism, community, and self-determination—whether at work, in the family, or in the schools—which have been the historic unfulfilled promise of the word *democracy*.

17

The New History

As I write this in 1996, the guardians of the "old history" are angry. Their heroes (Christopher Columbus, Andrew Jackson, Theodore Roosevelt, Woodrow Wilson, the giants of industry, and various military heroes) are increasingly being viewed as racists, militarists, and exploiters of labor. Indians, blacks, women, working people are getting more attention, their point of view listened to more closely. Twenty years ago, when I wrote the following article, a "new history" was just beginning to emerge, stimulated by the protest movements of the Sixties. This appeared in the *Boston Globe*, December 20, 1974, under the title "History Writing Changes."

There is a healthy change in the writing of history these days. We are hearing more from the bottom layers of society, so long submerged and silent under the volumes of memoirs produced by the political elite, and the histories written by intellectuals.

Out of the pages of a new book, *All God's Dangers*, an uneducated black man, Nate Shaw, speaks to us of his life, with enormous wisdom, with the rhythms of the southern earth in his language.

And we are listening now to those we thought dead. In Dee Brown's *Bury My Heart at Wounded Knee*, Chief Joseph challenges the intruder: "Perhaps you think the Creator sent you here to dispose of us as you see fit." And Red Cloud tells of the massacre of his people.

The graffiti has moved from the walls. It is a prison break. Tommy Trantino, a poet and artist in prison for life, starts his "Lock the Lock" with an unforgettable account of his first-grade encounter with the law: "The Lore of the Lamb."

Women, speaking out of the past, tell their hidden history in Eve Merriam's collection of memoirs, *Growing Up Female in America*. And the new Feminist Press publishes old-time treasures like "Life in the Iron Mills."

Working people talk honestly to Studs Terkel, who records their voices in *Hard Times* and *Working*.

Why are we now getting more history from below? Perhaps because of the tumult of social movements in America these past 15 years. Perhaps because we have less faith these days in the words of the famous. Now we are offended by Kissinger's definition of history, in his book *A World Restored*, in which he writes, "History is the memory of states."

To read the history of the Vietnam War from Kissinger's standpoint, the American troops were withdrawn and the truce was signed as a result of shrewd diplomacy (his own, of course) in Paris.

Such history would not only ignore the amazing resistance of the Vietnamese peasant to the most powerful military machine in the world. It would wipe out of our memories the huge movement against the war which grew in this country between 1965 and 1970. By 1968, half the draftees in northern California were failing to report for induction. One day in 1969, October 15, Moratorium Day, two million Americans gathered in thousands of places all over the country to protest the war. The movement spread into the armed forces, with GIs on patrol in Vietnam wearing black armbands of protest.

Mr. Nixon said the protesters had no effect on him. But the Pentagon Papers, not meant for public eyes, told the story: that in early 1968, the Johnson Administration was turned around in its escalation policy, not only by the Vietnamese spirit, but also by fear of the growing resistance to the war at home. And the Watergate record shows Mr. Nixon so undone by opposition that he became near-hysterical at the sight of one picketer near the White House.

It is good that we are getting more history from below. We have believed too long in our own helplessness, and the new history tells us how, sometimes, movements of people who don't seem to have much power can shake the rich and the powerful. Even out of their seats of power. Even into the prisoner's dock which they prepared for others.

18

The Marines
and the University

In early 1972 the war in Vietnam was going full blast. Boston University's new president, John Silber, invited the Marine Corps to come to the campus to recruit students for the Marines. Anti-war students and faculty decided to block the entrance to the building where the recruiting was to take place, and Silber called the police to arrest them. I was at home that week, sick with the flu, but when I heard from some of the participants what happened, I decided to write about the incident, especially to answer the argument, posed by Silber and others, that to interfere with Marine recruiting on campus was to violate civil liberties. My article was printed in the alternative newspaper, the *Boston Phoenix*, in early April, 1972, entitled "Silber, the University, and the Marines," and then was reprinted as a special supplement to the student newspaper, the *B.U. News*, as well as in several other publications.

What happened at Boston University on Monday, March 27, in front of the Placement Office, was a classic incident of what our textbooks call, without humor, "civilization." There were the young people (and a few older ones) protesting the violence of war, obstructively, nonviolently. There were the police, dispersing, clubbing, arresting them. There was the court intellectual patiently explaining to the world that the actions of the police were necessary to protect "freedom" or the "open" society or "respect for the law." (Our textbooks almost never report such incidents, which recur frequently in the history of civilization; they dwell on more romantic events—the Renaissance, the Reformation, the Bill of Rights, the rise of parliamentary democracy.)

The actors in the Boston University affair could not be better cast. The United States Marine Corps, whose business abroad is mass murder, played a benign employment agency. The Boston Tactical Police, whose business is brutality, played the role of protector of the community. And Boston University's President John Silber, whose business is obfuscation, played the role of educator.

There is not much to say about the Tactical Police Force; they look like and act like what they are. There is a bit more to say about the U.S. Marine Corps, especially because it is presented to us by Silber and the B.U. Public Relations Office (citing the words of a University Council statement of 1970) as one of several "legally constituted organizations from the field of education, government, social services and business" who offer "meaningful and satisfactory employment."

There is a good deal to say about John Silber doing what some intellectuals have done throughout history—finding a comfortable protected niche which the going order is willing to finance, in return for filling the heads of the younger generation with the most important lessons that the order wants them to learn (never mind the courses on Kant, Spinoza, and Marx; on Tolstoy, Joyce, and Faulkner, on history and politics and sociology; they are out front, but secondary). That lesson, taught crassly in grade school and high school, more sophisticatedly in college, is: respect for authority. The headline in B.U.'s official administration newspaper, *Currents*, reads: "Disruptive Students Must Be Taught Respect For Law, Says Dr. Silber."

It is true that one crucial function of the schools is training people to take the jobs that society has to offer—in business, government, or the military—so that the assembly lines of profit and death, whether blue-collar or intellectual, may be manned and the society kept going as is. But the much more important function of organized education is to teach the new generation that rule without which the leaders could not possibly carry on wars, ravage the country's wealth, keep down rebels and dissenters: the rule of obedience to legal authority. And no one can do that more skillfully, more convincingly, than the professional intellectual. A philosopher turned university president is best of all. If his arguments don't work on the ignorant students—who sometimes prefer to look at the world around them than to read Kant—then he can call in the police, and after that momentary interruption (the billy club serving as exclamation point to the rational argument) the discussion can continue, in a more subdued atmosphere.

But let us spend a little time on the United States Marine Corps. The rest of our discussion depends very much on who they are and what they do. John Silber would rather not bring up the Marines; this is understandable because they are an embarrassing burden for anyone to bear.

Of all the branches of the military, the Marines are the purest specialists in invading and occupying other countries; they have been called on again and again to do the dirty work of the American Empire. All through the twentieth century, they have been the storm troops of United States intervention in Latin America. It was under

Woodrow Wilson, an intellectual and university president, who entered the White House in 1913, that the Marines did some of their most ruthless work. In 1915, they invaded Haiti to put down a rebellion against the brutal military dictatorship of Vilbrun Sam, and incidentally to do a favor for the National City Bank of New York and other banking interests. The Haitians resisted, and the Marines killed 2,000 of them as part of a "pacification" program, after which Haiti came under American military and economic control. The following year, Marines invaded the Dominican Republic to help put down an insurrection there, and remained as an occupying force.

By 1924, the economic activities of half of the twenty Latin American countries were being directed by the United States. "Law and order" were necessary to allow the normal financial operations to continue without interruption. When rebellion broke out in 1926 in Nicaragua (where from 1912 to 1925 a legation guard of American Marines had stood watch in the Nicaraguan capital) "American fruit and lumber companies sent daily protests to the State Department," according to the Council on Foreign Relations. The following year, President Coolidge sent 5,000 Marines to put down the rebels.

More recently, in 1958, President Eisenhower sent 14,000 Marines into Lebanon (twice the size of the Lebanese army), and it must be said that oil was somewhere on his mind. And when a rebellion broke out in the Dominican Republic in 1965 against the military regime there, Lyndon Johnson sent the Marines. (On television one evening, the American public watched a Marine sergeant shooting in the back a man in Santo Domingo who was kicking garbage into the street). The dispatch of Marines had been urged several years before by Senator George Smathers, a close friend of the Kennedy-Johnson administrations and of business interests in Latin America, who said at the time: "Many Americans, having invested $250 million in the Dominican Republic, believe that Generalissimo Trujillo was the best guarantee of American interests in the country...open intervention must now be considered to protect their property and to prevent a communist coup."

In Vietnam, the Marines have participated in the general destruction of that country. They have shot civilians, burned villages, and contributed heavily to this country's shame. A dispatch to the *Washington Evening Star* (August 4, 1965) reported:

> This week Marines teamed with South Vietnamese troops to overrun the Viet Cong-dominated village of Chan Son, 10 miles south of Da Nang. Among 25 persons they killed were a woman and four children.
> Two of the children died at the hands of a young Marine who tossed a grenade into a village air raid shelter.

William R. Corson, a Marine colonel in Vietnam, has written about the Marines' search-and-destroy missions:

> There have been many thousands of search-and-destroy missions in Vietnam since the spring of 1965. Each of these operations has its own sad story to tell in terms of the almost total disregard for their effect on the Vietnamese people. Search-and-destroy tactics against VC-controlled areas have degenerated into savagery...

Corson wrote of Marine and ARVN units forcing 13,000 Vietnamese, almost all old men, women, and children, from Trung Luong, "Without a shot being fired, we had conspired with the ARVN to literally destroy the hopes, aspirations, and emotional stability of 13,000 human beings. This was not and is not war—it is genocide."

John Silber would like to avoid discussing the Marines. Philosophers are sometimes annoyed by the intrusion of facts into comfortably vague generalizations. He says, "We're going to operate a free campus here, so that students who are interested in acquiring information on a variety of jobs may find that information available

on this campus...I feel obligated to defend the open campus policy."
One would think from the statement by Silber after the Placement
Office events that students were protesting the recruitment of Fuller
Brush salesmen, instead of men to burn huts, kill peasants, invade
other countries. Silber wants us to forget that, and so he talks abstract-
ly about the "open campus." But it is part of rational inquiry to examine the empirical content of concepts. Let's look at the "open campus":

The campus is not and never has been open, so the term is fraud-
ulent. Not all organizations are given space to recruit; the very language of the University Council statement sets standards for recruiting—"legally constituted organizations" from certain fields; that pro-
vides a basis for exclusion. ("SDS has lost its privilege to schedule
facilities on the Boston University campus." Dean Staton Curtis.) Not
every professor is allowed to teach a course at Boston University; there
are standards (academic and other kinds). Not all students are allowed
to register; there are requirements (academic and financial). Not all
courses are allowed to get credit; there are criteria set by the Academic
Policy Committee. Not even all cars are allowed on the parking lot;
there are fees and qualifications.

It is nonsense for the administration to pretend that we must let
all organizations recruit or none; what is human intelligence for if not
to make distinctions? Would the Placement Office schedule interviews
for a company that announced its jobs open to "whites only"? Would
the Housing Office list apartments by landlords who discriminated by
race or religion? Indeed, the University does make distinctions, in
dozens of ways, some justifiable, others not. But to speak blithely of
an "open campus" is to distort the truth and to substitute slogans for
rational thought.

There is enough historical experience with such slogans to make
us suspicious. The term "free enterprise" used by the National
Association of Manufacturers meant freedom for corporations at the

expense of consumers. The term "freedom of contract" used by the Supreme Court in the early part of this century meant freedom for employers at the expense of women and children working sixty hours a week. The term "Open Door" used by President McKinley meant freedom for the United States to despoil China just as the other powers had done. And the term "open campus" used by John Silber means freedom for the Marines and Dow Chemical and Lockheed Aircraft (all "legally constituted organizations") to find the personnel to keep the war and the military-industrial machine going.

Here is Silber:

> We have made it perfectly clear that there is no immunity on this campus from the common and statutory law of the United States or the Commonwealth of Massachusetts. These laws are in effect, and Boston University will cooperate in enforcing these laws.

Is not respect for human life more important than respect for law? Why did not Silber say instead (telling the Marines to go elsewhere): "We have made it perfectly clear that there is no immunity on this campus from the laws of humanity, which say Thou Shall Not Kill." It is sad that a university president, presumably committed to rational inquiry, should make "respect for the law" his supreme value. It is a standard which shows ethical impoverishment and intellectual laziness.

The truth is that John Silber does not believe in an open campus. It is just that he wants to be the doorkeeper; he wants to set the standards for who may use the University. The pretense of an open campus is to avoid having to reveal his standards, because they are not easily defensible. They are not moral ones—not standards based on a concern for human beings—not when he opens the campus to the Marines. His standards are legal ones ("legally constituted organizations"). If you are lethal but legal, you will be welcome at Boston

University; if you are nonviolent but illegal, the police will be called out to disperse you (violently). Silber's standard of legality is appropriate, not for the independent thinker in a democracy, but for the obsequious servant of the overbearing state.

Thus, the apparently absolute and attractive principle of the "open campus" is not what it seems. We cannot accept abstract principles without examining their specific content, without asking: what standards are being used, what distinctions are being made? Would we accept the principle of "open skies" without asking if this includes being open to planes carrying hydrogen bombs over populated cities? Would we accept "open riverways" without asking if this means being open to radioactive wastes, or "open streets" without asking if this means being open to cars driving sixty miles an hour past children playing?

The problem, which Silber either does not see or does not want to see, is that any valid principle (like "openness," or "freedom," or "security") when made an absolute, clashes with other principles equally valid. Somebody's liberty may clash with another person's security. Somebody's right to recruit personnel may clash with another person's right to live. As Zechariah Chafee put it, "Your right to swing your fist stops where my nose begins." To hold to any one principle like the "open campus" ignoring other values, is simplistic thinking; it also contains the seeds of fanaticism. John Silber, in the current B.U. situation, has shown elements of both.

A rational and human view would balance one ethical principle against others. This cannot be done in the abstract; it can only be done by looking into the factual content of a specific situation. If there is a "right to protest," and a "right to an open campus," there is no way of deciding a conflict between them *on ethical grounds*, without inquiring more closely: who is protesting and how and at what cost to human life and liberty; who is recruiting, and with what consequences for human beings? The one sure way of evading a decision on ethical grounds, and thus saving the job of investigating the facts, is to make the decision on *legal* grounds. This is what Silber has done. This avoidance of ethical issues is expected from policemen, but not from philosophers. To rest on the law, one need not inquire into the history and current behavior of the Marine Corps, into the shattered villages, the burned bodies of the Vietnamese people.

Even inside Silber's legalistic framework, however, empty as it is of human and moral content, there is a troublesome discrepancy. If he is so concerned with "respect for the law," how can he ignore the fact that the Marine Corps is recruiting for an illegal war, a war carried on outside the Constitution by the President and the military, in violation of a half-dozen international treaties signed by the United States? The only difference between the Marines recruiting and Murder, Inc. recruiting (aside from the scale of their violence) is that the lawlessness of the Marines is "legal" in the sense that the authorities, involved themselves in the same crimes, will not prosecute. What hypocrisy there is in the injunction "respect the law!"

When John Silber was asked at a press conference whether he would allow Nazis to recruit on campus, he evaded the issue by talking about the right of Nazis to *speak.* But the distinction between free speech and free action is a very important one. By muddying the distinction, Silber is able to transfer to actions like recruiting for war that immunity from regulation that we all want for free speech. But while there are gray areas between speech and action, recruiting is not in that area: the fact that it is accompanied by speech makes it no more an exercise in free speech than a meeting by corporate heads to fix prices, or the instructions of Captain Medina to move into the hamlet of My Lai.

Freedom of speech should be virtually absolute; this is not because it is not subject to the idea that competing values must be measured against one another for their human consequences, but because in the case of speech the measuring is easy. Free speech is in itself a valuable social good, and it is extremely rare that the exchange of ideas—no matter how wrong or even vicious certain ideas may be—creates such an immediate danger to any person's life or liberty as to warrant regulating it. (The Supreme Court, however, in its patriotic fervor, has often found immediate danger in radicals and pacifists passing out their literature.)

Speech is one thing. Activities which affect the health or liberty or lives of others, including the activities of business organizations and military organizations, are another matter. John Silber has talked much recently about "civilization and barbarism." But is not war the greatest barbarism? Would not a civilization worthy of the name, while absolutely respecting the free exchange of ideas, halt the aggressive violence of the military? Would not a decent university, while maintaining a campus open to all ideas, take a stand for human life against those who have violated it on such a frightful scale (the dead in Vietnam number over a million)?

Those words against the war which John Silber delivered at his inauguration remain empty so long as he does not act against the war when he has an opportunity to do so. How small a gesture, and yet what a lesson in defiance it would be for 15,000 B.U. students, if Silber would say to the Marines: "Do your dirty work elsewhere." Cannot a university president match the courage of the young men who have said to the military: we refuse to be inducted—or the courage of the men in the military who have said: we refuse to kill? Those young people, those GIs, acted illegally, but honorably. If John Silber seeks the safety that legality affords, he can have it, but only at the price of dishonor.

Silber: "...students must be taught...that the real issue is not ideology but respect for law." Is it possible that Silber does not know the chief social function of law has been, in the United States as elsewhere, to maintain the existing structure of privilege and property? Does he not know that the socialization of young people in obedience to law helps keep within the most narrow bounds any attempts to create a truly just society? Does he not know that "the law" cannot be sacred to anyone concerned with moral values, that it is not made by God but by fallible, interest-ridden legislators, and enforced by corrupt prosecutors and judges? Does he not know that the law weighs heaviest on the poor, the black, the social critics, and lightest on the corporate interests, the politically powerful? Does he not know that the police commit assault and battery repeatedly, and the President of the United States is responsible for the murder of hundreds of thousands of people? Does he not know that the law will never take the biggest lawbreakers to task because they are the ones who control the law, and they will use it instead against anti-war priests and nuns, black militants, and student protesters? Does he not understand that "respect for the law" as a supreme value is one of the chief characteristics of the totalitarian society?

Silber does not talk about the right of civil disobedience. He insists, however, that it stay within the rules laid down by the authorities (of which he is one) when the very spirit of civil disobedience is defiance of authority. He acts surprised when students blocking the Marine recruiters do not walk voluntarily to the police wagons. He seems not to understand that not every advocate of civil disobedience shares his limited definition of it. He invokes Socrates as one who insisted on going along with his own punishment because he felt a basic obligation to Athens. But, in the spirit of free inquiry, we may ask if Socrates was not, in those moments of debate with Crito, absurdly subservient to the power of the state. Should we model ourselves on Socrates (that is, on Plato, who put the words in Socrates' mouth) at his most jingoistic moment, saying about one's country that one must "obey in silence if it orders you to endure flogging or imprisonment, or it sends you to battle to be wounded or to die."

John Silber did not even seem to be embarrassed as he invoked the name of Martin Luther King, claiming that King "emphasized the importance of showing respect for lawfulness at the same time that he refused to abide by a specific law." That is a gross distortion. It is true that King went to jail rather than escaping, but it isn't at all clear that he did this out of any overall respect for "lawfulness" rather than out of tactical and dramatic motives, or simply out of lack of choice. I doubt that King would criticize Angela Davis or Daniel Berrigan, who carried their defiance of authority beyond that point of arrest, who refused to surrender to the government because they believed its activities did not deserve respect. It is true that King urged respect for his opponents and love for all fellow beings, but it is not true that he "emphasized...respect for lawfulness." I knew Martin Luther King, and was with him on occasions of civil disobedience, in Alabama and Georgia, and it is a disservice to his memory to twist his views so as to omit what was by far his chief emphasis: resistance to immoral authority.

Would Martin Luther King have equated the "violence" of sitting on the steps of the Placement Office (so much like the sit-ins of black students in segregated restaurants, which were also disruptive and illegal) with the violence of the government in war? When Silber said after the Placement office event, "We are not going to be intimidated by brute force and brute violence," he showed a shocking absence of that most essential quality of the intelligent, rational person: a sense of proportion. King was against violence, but he did have a sense of proportion. In his last years, he decided that he would not condemn the violence of black uprisings in the ghetto, before taking into account the record of violence by the United States government. Listen to him, speaking at Riverside Church in New York, April 4, 1967:

> ...I knew that I could never again raise my voice against the violence of the oppressed in the ghettos without having first spoken clearly to the greatest purveyor of violence in the world today—my own government.

How odd that a man whose own behavior that day at the Placement Office more closely resembled that of Birmingham's Bull Connor—replete with police dogs, hidden photographers, and club-wielding police—should invoke the name of Martin Luther King, who would have been there on the steps with the students.

The idea that one who commits civil disobedience must "willingly" accept punishment is an oft-repeated but fallacious notion. Silber repeatedly confuses "community" and "society" with government. He talks of "refusing to accept the penalties that go with violating the law" as showing "contempt for organized society." No, it is showing contempt for organized government, and that is justified when the government is behaving as badly as this one is. He talks of "the community...arresting and punishing them." It is not the community that arrests and punishes, but the legal authorities. The reason for showing contempt for government, for defying the law, is precisely because government and law show contempt for the lives and liberties of the community.

Silber talks of the "social contract" that we are supposed to have made with our government. Of course the government would like us to believe that such a contract exists, one binding us to obedience of the law and allowing the government to do as it pleases. It is as if Silber has not read, or has forgotten David Hume, back in the eighteenth century, who brought Locke back to earth and history by pointing out: "Almost all the governments which exist at present, or of which there remains any record in history, have been founded originally, either on usurpation or conquest, or both, without any pretense of a fair consent or voluntary subjection of the people." Silber talks as if we have some sort of obligation, based on a voluntary agreement, to obey the leaders who have taken us again and again into war, who have allowed a few to monopolize the enormous wealth of this country. Hume, a conservative but honest man, told it like it is: "Is there anything discoverable in all these events but force and violence? Where is the mutual agreement or voluntary association so much talked of?"

What Silber calls "civilization," what he thinks we have a "social contract" to obey, is the state and its agents. What he calls "barbarism" is the courage of those who resist the state. "It is important that civilization not acquiesce to barbarism...civilization doesn't abdicate before the threat of barbarism; rather it calls the police." When antiwar protestors represent "barbarism" and the Tactical Police represent "civilization," then we certainly need what Confucius suggested, a "rectification of names."

Here is Silber again (at the same press conference reported in the official *Currents*, from which the other quotations in this article are taken):

> We had recourse to the police power of the state. Every civilized country in the world has found it necessary to rely on police power to protect itself against the use of force and violence by individual members of that community. When one calls upon the properly designated institution to exercise that force, it can certainly be an expression of civilization.

In Silber's inaugural address, on "The Pollution of Time," he deplored ignorance of history. But does he not know from history that the "civilized" countries have used massive violence against one another (Guernica, Dachau, Coventry, Dresden, Hiroshima, Nagasaki, Budapest, My Lai) and the most brutal force against movements of protest and resistance inside their borders? Does he not know from history that the "properly designated" institutions have engaged in a thousand times more force and violence than any individuals or any social movement of opposition?

If the word "civilization" can be given some positive moral content, it should mean the attempts of man to create a society in which the violence of war, and persecution by class or race or sex, are resisted and restrained, so that they can be ultimately eliminated. By such a definition, students blocking the recruiting of soldiers to kill Vietnamese peasants truly represent civilization; those who attack them, and those who order the attack, represent barbarism.

Does John Silber—bright, well-read, articulate, energetic—not understand these points about history, about nation-states, about the law, about morality, about war, about social protest? We are always surprised when educated people don't understand simple, clear concepts, but that is because the brightest people strain their perceptions through a mesh of interest, position, role. It didn't matter that McGeorge Bundy was "brilliant" from elementary school throughout graduate school and beyond; his vision was distorted by his position in the Establishment, his closeness to power, and he ended up supporting the most stupid, as well as the most immoral of policies in Vietnam.

Silber came to Boston University with strong ideas about academic "excellence," and enormous drive, determined to make the University "first-rate." But education is not a technological problem; it is more a matter of human relationships and moral concern. Academic excellence, in a context of amorality, does not have much meaning. Mussolini made the trains run on time; but the importance of that petered out on the sands of Ethiopia. Boston University cannot be a place of *moral* excellence, if it is run by a dictatorship, however efficient that dictatorship is.

What would a truly free campus be like? It would give absolute freedom to the exchange of ideas, of all kinds. It would insist on its own freedom from the power of government, of donors and trustees. It would not bow to law and authority; not to the authority of the President of the United States or to the authority of the President of the University. Its academic decisions would be made by faculty and students; staff and maintenance workers would share in decisions about the allocation of the university's money. The president and deans would carry out the decisions, as administrators constantly accountable to faculty, students and staff. The university's courses would be open to anyone, whether they could pay or not.

A truly free university would not celebrate obedience, for obedience is what has enabled governments to send young men by the millions to die in war. It would celebrate resistance and disobedience, because the world, so full of authoritarianism, so full of policemen, so racked with injustice and violence, needs rebels badly. It would admire not that technical intellectual efficiency which ignores the fate of human beings far away or near, but that combination of sense and sensibility one finds in good people everywhere, educated or not. It would understand that the most important thing about a university is not its programs or curricula or any of the accoutrements of the upward-striving educator, but its soul.

19

Secrecy, Archives, and the Public Interest

In 1970 I was invited to give a paper at the annual meeting of the Society of American Archivists in Washington D.C. My paper was entitled "The Archivist & The New Left," and was published a number of years later (1977) in a journal, *The Midwestern Archivist*. In introducing my article, the editor said: "Professor Howard Zinn shocked and offended many in his audience...[but] it was welcomed most enthusiastically by a relatively small group of mainly younger archivists who thereafter committed themselves to publicizing Zinn's views and persuading their colleagues of the validity of his criticisms of the archival profession. Largely as a consequence of Zinn's challenge, a small number of archivists in San Francisco the following year...founded ACT, an informal caucus dedicated to reform within both the Society of American Archivists and the archival profession."

L et me work my way in from the great circle of the world to us at the center by discussing, in turn, three things: the social role of the professional in modern times; the scholar in the United States today; and the archivist here and now.

I will start by quoting from a document—an insidious move to gain rapport with archivists, some might say, except that the document is a bit off the beaten track in archival work (a fact we might ponder later). It is the transcript of a trial that took place in Chicago in the fall of 1969, called affectionately "the Conspiracy Trial." I refer to it because the transcript occasionally touches on the problem of the professional person—whether a lawyer, historian, or archivist—and the relation between professing one's craft and professing one's humanity. On October 15, 1969, the day of the national Moratorium to protest the war in Vietnam, defense attorney William Kunstler wore a black armband in court to signify his support of the Moratorium and his protest against the war. The government's lawyer, Thomas Foran, called this to the attention of the judge, saying: "Your Honor, that's outrageous. This man is a mouthpiece. Look at him, wearing a band like his clients, your Honor."

The day before the Moratorium, Attorney Kunstler had asked the court to recess October 15 to observe the Moratorium. This dialogue between Kunstler and Judge Hoffman then followed:

> Mr. Kunstler:...And I think it is as important, your Honor, to protest more than some thirty thousand American deaths and Lord knows how many Vietnamese deaths that have occurred in that country as it is to mourn one man (Eisenhower) in the United States, and if courts can close for the death of one man who lived a full life, they ought to be closed for the deaths of thousands and millions of innocent people whose lives have been corrupted and rotted and perverted by this utter horror that goes on in your name and my name...
>
> The Court: Not in my name.
>
> Mr. Kunstler: It is in your name, too, in the name of the people of the United States.

The Court: You just include yourself. Don't join me with you. Goodness.
Don't you and I...

Mr. Kunstler: You are me, your Honor, because every citizen...you are a citizen and I am a citizen.

The Court: Only because you are a member of the bar of this court and I
am obliged to hear you respectfully, as I have done.

Mr. Kunstler: No, your Honor, you are more than that. You are a citizen
of the United States.

The Court: Yes, I am.

Mr. Kunstler: And I am a citizen of the United States, and it is done in our
name, in Judge Hoffman's name and William Kunstler's name.

The Court: That will be all, sir. I shall hear you no further.

Kunstler was trying to accomplish something very difficult, to get
a judge to emerge from that comfortable corner which society had
declared as his natural habitat, and to declare himself a citizen, even
while on the bench, in his robes, plying his profession. Kunstler said a
slaughter was taking place in Vietnam, and it was going on in the name
of all citizens, and he wanted the Judge to recognize that fact not only
in the evening at home after his robes were off, or at the country club
on the weekend, but there, in his daily work, in his most vital hours,
in the midst of his job of judging. Kunstler failed, but his attempt illustrates the tension all of us feel, if we have not been totally mesmerized
by the grandeur of our position, the tension between our culture-
decreed role as professionals and our existential needs as human beings.

Professionalism is a powerful form of social control. By professionalism I mean the almost total immersion in one's craft, being so
absorbed in the day-to-day exercise of those skills, as to have little
time, energy, or will to consider what part those skills play in the total
social scheme. I say *almost-total* immersion, because if it were total, we
would be suspicious of it. Being not quite total, we are tolerant of it,
or at least sufficiently confused by the mixture to do nothing. It is
something like Yossarian's jaundice, in *Catch 22*, where Joseph Heller
writes:

> Yossarian was in the hospital with a pain in his liver that fell just short of being jaundice. If it became jaundice they could treat it. If it didn't become jaundice and went away they could discharge him. But this just being short of jaundice all the time confused them.

By social control I mean maintaining things as they are, preserving traditional arrangements, preventing any sharp change in how the society distributes wealth and power. Both in pre-modern and modern times, the basic combination for social control has remained the same: force and deception. Machiavelli, writing on the threshold of the modern era, drew upon the past to prescribe for the future that same combination: the power of the lion, the shrewdness of the fox. The modern era has magnified enormously both elements: it has concentrated force more efficiently than ever before and it has used more sophisticated techniques for deception. The printing press, heralding the spread of knowledge to large sections of the population, made large-scale deception both necessary and possible, and in the last four centuries we have progressed from the printing press to color television, from Machiavelli to Herman Kahn.

There were few professionals in the old days. Now they are everywhere, and their skills, their knowledge, could be a threat to the status quo. But their will to challenge the going order is constantly weakened by rewards of money and position. And they are so divided, so preoccupied with their particular specialties, as to spend most of their time smoothing, tightening their tiny piece of linkage in the social machine. This leaves very little time or energy to worry about whether the machine is designed for war or peace, for social need or individual profits, to help us or to poison us.

This specialization of modern times is pernicious enough for waiters, auto mechanics, and doctors, and the bulk of the workers in society, who contribute to the status quo without even knowing it, simply by keeping the vast machinery going without a hitch. But certain professionals serve the status quo in special ways. Weapons experts, or scientists in military research, may be enormously gifted in their own fields, yet so constricted in their role as citizens, as to turn over their frighteningly potent products without question or with very feeble questioning, to whatever uses the leaders of society decide. Remember the role of the humane genius, Robert Oppenheimer, in the decision to drop the atomic bomb on Hiroshima. Oppenheimer was a member of the Scientific Advisory Panel which recommended the dropping of the bomb in Hiroshima, thinking it was necessary to save lives. But Oppenheimer later commented (his testimony is in the files of the AEC):

> We didn't know beans about the military situation in Japan. We didn't know whether they could be caused to surrender by other means or whether the invasion was really inevitable.

Equally important for social control as the military scientists, are those professionals who are connected with the dissemination of knowledge in society: the teachers, the historians, the political scientists, the journalists, and yes, the archivists. Here too, professionalization leads to impotence, as everyone is given a little corner of the playground. And it is considered unprofessional to organize everyone in the yard to see if the playground director is violating various of the Ten Commandments as we play. We have all heard the cries of "don't politicize our profession" when someone asks joint action on the war in Vietnam. This has the effect of leaving only our spare time for political checking-up while those who make the political decisions in society—this being their profession—work at it full time.

The neat separation, keeping your nose to the professional grindstone, and leaving politics to your left-over moments, assumes that your profession is not inherently political. It is neutral. Teachers are objective and unbiased. Textbooks are eclectic and fair. The historian is even-handed and factual. The archivist keeps records, a scrupulously neutral job. And so it goes, as Kurt Vonnegut says.

However, if any of these specialists in the accumulation and dissemination of knowledge were to walk over to another part of the playpen, the one marked political sociology, they could read Karl Mannheim, who in *Ideology and Utopia*, points out (following Marx, of course, but it is more prudent to cite Mannheim) that knowledge has a social origin and social use. It comes out of a divided, embattled world, and is poured into such a world. It is not neutral either in origin or effect. It reflects the biases of a diverse social order, but with one important qualification: that those with the most power and wealth in society will dominate the field of knowledge, so that it serves their interests. The scholar may swear to his neutrality on the job, but whether he be physicist, historian, or archivist, his work will tend, in this theory, to maintain the existing social order by perpetuating its values, by legitimizing its priorities, by justifying its wars, perpetuating its prejudices, contributing to its xenophobia, and apologizing for its class order. Thus Aristotle, behind that enormous body of philosophical wisdom, justifies slavery, and Plato, underneath that dazzling set of dialogues, justifies obedience to the state, and Machiavelli, respected as one of the great intellectual figures of history, urges our concentration on means rather than ends.

Now maybe we have not been oblivious to this idea that the professional scholars in any society tend to buttress the existing social order and values of that society. But we have tended to attribute this to other societies, or other times or other professions. Not the United States. Now now. Not here. Not us. It was easy to detect the control of the German scholars or the Russian scholars, but much harder to recognize that the high school texts of our own country have fostered jingoism, war heroes, the Sambo approach to the black man, the vision of the Indian as savage, and the notion that white Western

Civilization is the cultural, humanistic summit of man's time on earth.

We could see where scholars in Nazi Germany or Soviet Russian, by quietly doing their job, would be perpetuating an awful set of conditions; to keep *that* kind of social order intact, and we hoped intellectuals would rebel. The U.S. however, was a different matter; what was wrong here was not the social order itself, but problems at the margins of it. It was all right for intellectuals to keep this basically decent order intact by doing our jobs; and we could attack the problems at the margins by signing petitions and joining political campaigns after hours.

Events of the past decade, I would now argue, have begun to challenge that complacency, that part-time commitment to political involvement which assumes a basically just society, needing only marginal reforms. We have won those reforms. The U.S. is the great model in history of the reformist nation, and the past half-century has been labeled by one of our important historians as "The Age of Reform." We have had New Deal legislation to take care of our economic flaws, Civil Rights laws to take care of our racial problems, Supreme Court decisions to expand our rights in court, the Good Neighbor Policy, Marshall Plan, and Alliance for Progress to humanize our relations with other countries.

Yet, it is exactly at the crest of these reforms that the United States has found itself in a turbulent internal crisis in which a significant part of the younger generation has begun to question the legitimacy of the government, the values of the culture. How is it that after a barrage of Supreme Court decisions, Civil Rights laws, the confrontation between black and white in this country is at its most intense? How is it that after the New Freedom, the New Deal, the Fair Deal, the New Frontier, and the Great Society, the distribution of the immense resources of this society is at its most irrational, its most wasteful?

The problems of the United States are not peripheral and have not been met by our genius at reform. They are not the problems of excess, but of normalcy. Our racial problem is not the Ku Klux Klan or the South, but our fundamental liberal assumption that paternalism solves all. Our economic problem is not a depression but the normal functioning of the economy, dominated by corporate power and profit. Our problem with justice is not a corrupt judge or bribed jury but the ordinary day-to-day functioning of the police, the law, the courts, where property rights come before human rights. Our problem in foreign policy is not a particular mad adventure: the Spanish American War or the Vietnam War, but a continuous set of suppositions about our role in the world, involving missionary imperialism, and a belief in America's ability to solve complex social problems.

If all this is so, then the *normal* functioning of the scholar, the intellectual, the researcher, helps maintain those corrupt norms in the United States, just as the intellectual in Germany, Soviet Russia, or South Africa, by simply doing his small job, maintains what is normal in those societies. And if so, then what we always asked of scholars in those terrible places is required of us in the United States today: rebellion against the *norm*.

In the United States, however, the contribution of scholars to the status quo is more subtle and more complex than in more blatantly oppressive societies. Only a small number of scholars give direct service to the war. Most simply go about their scholarly business, their acts of commission subtle, their acts of omission gross. For instance, the historian's emphasis on presidents and laws only subtly perpetuates an elitist approach to politics; missing completely in Morison's *Oxford History of the American People* is the Ludlow Massacre of 1914. The political scientists' emphasis on electoral politics only subtly *suggests* that voting is the central problem in democratic control: you look in vain for extensive work on the politics of protest. The scholar's emphasis on Supreme Court decisions only subtly distorts the fact of constitutional rights; constitutional histories omit the reality of police power in determining how much free expression there really is on the streets.

The archivist, even more than the historian and the political scientist, tends to be scrupulous about his neutrality, and to see his job as a technical job, free from the nasty world of political interest: a job of collecting, sorting, preserving, making available, the records of the society. But I will stick by what I have said about other scholars, and argue that the archivist, in subtle ways, tends to perpetuate the political and economic status quo simply by going about his ordinary business. His supposed neutrality is, in other words, a fake. If so, the rebellion of the archivist against his normal role is not, as so many scholars fear, the politicizing of a neutral craft, but the humanizing of an inevitably political craft. Scholarship in society is inescapably political. Our choice is not between being political or not. Our choice is to follow the politics of the going order, that is, to do our job within the priorities and directions set by the dominant forces of society, or else to promote those human values of peace, equality, and justice, which our present society denies.

I would guess from my small experience—and I leave it up to you to carry on the discussion from there—that the following points are true:

(1) That the existence, preservation, and availability of archives, documents, records in our society are very much determined by the distribution of wealth and power. That is, the most powerful, the richest elements in society have the greatest capacity to find documents, preserve them, and decide what is or is not available to the public. This means government, business, and the military are dominant.

(2) That one of the ways in which information is controlled and democracy denied, is by the government withholding important documents from the public, or keeping secret their existence altogether, or censoring them (how we must struggle to get data about the Gulf of Tonkin, the Bay of Pigs, the bombing of Laos, CIA operations in

Guatemala). And that while the ostensible purpose of such secrecy is the physical security of the nation, the actual purpose is almost always the political security of those who run the nation. Ernest May writes in *A Case for Court Historians*:

> The materials needed by historians would also contain much information which, on other than security grounds, government officials would prefer not to see released... Sec'y of State Rusk could conceivably have been embarrassed by revelations about advice he gave when Asst. Sec'y of State in the Truman Administration...

(3) That the collection of records, papers, and memoirs, as well as oral history, is biased towards the important and powerful people of the society, tending to ignore the impotent and obscure: we learn most about the rich, not the poor; the successful, not the failures; the old, not the young; the politically active, not the politically alienated; men, not women; white, not black; free people rather than prisoners; civilians rather than soldiers; officers rather than enlisted men. Someone writing about Strom Thurmond will have no problem with material. But what if someone wants to write about the blind black jazz pianist, Art Tatum?

(4) That, despite the recent development of oral history, the written word still dominates, and this tends to emphasize the top layers, the most literate elements in the population.

(5) That the emphasis in the collection of records is towards individuals rather than movements, towards static interviews, rather than the dynamics of social interaction in demonstrations. For instance, where is the raw material—that *very* raw material—on the experience of demonstrators in Chicago at the hands of the police at the 1968 convention, which was used by the Walker Commission? I wonder, for instance, if Boston University, proud that it holds the papers of Martin Luther King, has recorded the experience of students who were clubbed by police at the Student Union last year?

(6) That the emphasis is on the past over the present, on the anti-

quarian over the contemporary; on the non-controversial over the controversial; the cold over the hot. What about the transcripts of trials? Shouldn't these be made easily available to the public? Not just important trials like the Chicago Conspiracy Trial I referred to, but the ordinary trials of ordinary persons, an important part of the record of our society. Even the extraordinary trials of extraordinary persons are not available, but perhaps they do not show our society at its best. The trial of the Catonsville 9 would be lost to us if Father Daniel Berrigan had not gone through the transcript and written a play based on it.

(7) That far more resources are devoted to the collection and preservation of what already exists as records, than to *recording* fresh data: I would guess that more energy and money is going for the collection and publication of the Papers of John Adams than for recording the experiences of soldiers on the battlefront in Vietnam. Where are the interviews of Seymour Hersh with those involved in the My Lai Massacre, or Fred Gardner's interviews with those involved in the Presidio Mutiny Trial in California, or Wallace Terry's interviews with black GIs in Vietnam? Where are the recorded experiences of the young Americans in Southeast Asia who quit the International Volunteer Service in protest against American policy there, or of the Foreign Service officers who have quietly left?

Let me point to some random pieces of evidence to illustrate these points I have made about the going bias in archival work. Recently, I came across a list of letterpress publications sponsored, assisted, or endorsed by the National Historical Publications Commission of the General Services Administration. The papers of thirty-three Americans are being published. There is one black person on the list, and that is Booker T. Washington. What about Mother Jones, the labor organizer, or Bob Moses, the SNCC leader, or the papers of the man who lives down the street? I know that the very stress on collected papers is severely limiting, but there *are* papers of the leaders of protest movements. Of course there are problems: the papers of Big Bill Haywood were destroyed by the United States Government. But what of Eugene Debs or Clarence Darrow? I suppose it could be claimed that there is one important leader of a protest movement on the list: that is Jefferson Davis.

Another item of evidence: In an article by Amelia Fry and Willa Baum, oral historians at the University of California at Berkeley, the authors cite the lack of money as causing some oral history projects to erase important tapes. They note the feeling among some persons involved in oral history that "since preserving tapes is expensive and required special conditions, the decision should hinge on the affluence of the project and the relative importance of the person interviewed."

The Oral History Collection at Columbia University seems almost a caricature of the biases I have noted. It has long ignored the poor, the obscure, the radicals, the outcasts—it has ignored movements and living events. When I wrote from the South, in the midst of the civil rights movement, to the Columbia Oral History Collection to try to get them to tape what was happening at the time in Georgia, Alabama, Mississippi, I got a bureaucratic response which muttered about money and priorities and allocations, the upshot of which was: no. But the latest report of the Oral History Project gives doting attention to its Air Force Project, Navy Project, Marine Project. It is happy to have the reminiscences of General O'Donnell: how about the reminiscences of the various Yossarians in the Air Force? It has the Allan Nevins project, which consists of interviewing the friends of Allan Nevins. (Wouldn't it be more interesting to interview the enemies of Allan Nevins?) It will spend much time interviewing members of the Eisenhower Administration, based on a $120,000 grant from the National Archives. Has the Project interviewed Mrs. Fannie Lou Hamer of Ruleville, Mississippi, or Eldridge Cleaver or Dave Dellinger? Did it go to the Poor Peoples' March and interview the people camped out there in the mud? Has it interviewed Vietnam veterans in the rehabilitation hospitals? Does it go into the ghetto around Columbia University? Or is that job only for Kenneth Clark? For important contemporary interviews, one might do better to consult *Playboy Magazine* than the Columbia Oral History Project.

Another item of evidence: In the American Historical Association newsletter of April 1970, there is a report of the "Thirteenth Meeting of the Advisory Committee on '*Foreign Relations of the United States*,' a series of State Department documents issued by the year. The Advisory Committee has representatives of the American Historical Association, the American Political Science Association, and the Society of International Law. One clause in the report reads: "In 1962 the Secretary of State officially set the time lapse at 20 years; the committee cannot have access to these Foreign Relations documents until twenty years have elapsed. By what right, in a democracy requiring the enlightenment of the public, does any bureaucrat make such decisions for us all? Yet this advisory committee of scholars is painfully obsequious before the might of government: they complain that it takes as much as two years for the volumes of Foreign Relations to get clearance from Department of State, but instead of challenging the whole concept of clearance, the committee only asks humbly for the clearance procedure to move faster.

Note also that while the Foreign Relations staff must wait twenty years, the public at large must wait thirty years, and indeed the committee of scholars say they are "highly disturbed by the narrowing gap" between the scholars' wait and the public's wait, and by the possibility of "outside, *ad hoc* publication"—that is publication outside the official aegis of the State Department and the committee of scholars. Such publication, they warn, may beat the Foreign Relations series to the punch, and "provide inaccurate or partial accounts" which "may achieve a popular impact." This could be offset, however, by quicker publication of the Foreign Relations series, with the cooperation of the State Department. We find in it another paragraph of outstanding timidity, in which the committee expresses its concern that the open period may move back beyond 30 years. Such a move, the committee says with measured sycophancy, would be "violative of the commendable record the Department of State has maintained over the decades in making the foreign relations documentation of the United States publicly and systematically available." In that paragraph the committee notes that other countries such as England are moving in the opposite direction, decreasing the years of closed records, and then it concludes: "The committee is not herewith advocating advancing the open period for full public access to diplomatic documentation, but it believes that everything should be done to prevent it from being set back in excess of thirty years."

Thus, the committee falls all over itself in gratitude that the public only has to wait thirty years. It doesn't want to rock the boat (which all hands aboard know is sinking) by asking for a shorter wait. Where is the bold, inquiring spirit of the scholar in a democratic state, demanding to see government documents as a right, not a privilege? No wonder, with such a government, and with such scholars, we so desperately need I.F. Stone.

What is the net effect of the kind of archival biases I have just described? To protect governmental authorities from close scrutiny, and therefore from the indignation, the anger that might result from a closer look at government policies. To glorify important people, powerful people, military, political, and business leaders, to keep obscure the lives of ordinary people in the society. To maintain such archival biases requires no malfeasance on the part of archivists, only passivity, only falling into the lines already set by the dominant trends of the profession.

I say *dominant* trends, because I know there are some good things being done in archival work, some pioneering efforts in recording events, in oral history with ordinary people, in black history, in labor history. But let's resist the characteristically American trick of passing off fundamental criticism by pointing to a few reforms. The Saigon regime reformed itself for twenty years before it finally fell. We are still passing civil rights laws, and poverty bills. Let us not once again be happy because like Yossarian, we don't quite have jaundice. We also are not quite cured. Like Yossairian, we are still in the hospital. Like him, we are in danger. And we will remain in danger until, like him, we rebel.

I have argued that the crisis of present-day America is not one of aberration, but of normalcy, that at issue are not marginal characteristics, but our central operating values: the profit system, racial paternalism, violence towards those outside our narrow pale. If this is so, then scholarly passivity, far from being neutral and disinterested, serves those operating values. What is required then is to wrench ourselves out of our passivity, to try to integrate our professional lives with our humanity.

I have only two proposals for archivists: One, that they engage in a campaign to open all government documents to the public. If there are rare exceptions, let the burden of proof be on those who claim them, not as now on the citizen who wants information. And two, that they take the trouble to compile a whole new world of documentary material, about the lives, desires, needs, of ordinary people. Both of these proposals are in keeping with the spirit of democracy, which demands that the population know what the government is doing, and that the condition, the grievances, the will of the underclasses become a force in the nation.

To refuse to be instruments of social control in an essentially undemocratic society, to begin to play some small part in the creation of a real democracy: these are worthy jobs for historians, for archivists, for us all.

20

The Uses
of Scholarship

We were sad to hear of the death in 1996 of Mario Savio, leader in the Sixties of the "Free Speech Movement" at the University of California in Berkeley. It reminded us that the movements of that decade provoked a re-examination of the role of the university and the position of the scholar in a world needing radical change. The following essay appeared in the *Saturday Review* of October 18, 1969, under the title "The Case for Radical Change." It appeared also as the opening chapter in my book *The Politics of History*, "Knowledge As A Form Of Power."

It is time that we scholars began to earn our keep in this world. Thanks to a gullible public, we have been honored, flattered, even paid, for producing the largest number of inconsequential studies in the history of civilization: tens of thousands of articles, books, monographs, millions of term papers; enough lectures to deafen the gods.

Like politicians we have thrived on public innocence, with this difference: the politicians are paid for caring, when they really don't; we are
paid for not caring, when we really do.

Occasionally, we emerge from the library stacks to sign a petition
or deliver a speech, then return to produce even more of inconse-
quence. We are accustomed to keeping our social commitment
extracurricular and our scholarly work safely neutral. We were the first
to learn that awe and honor greet those who have flown off into space
while people suffer on earth.

If this accusation seems harsh, read the titles of doctoral disserta-
tions published in the past twenty years, and the pages of the leading
scholarly journals for the same period, alongside the lists of war dead,
the figures on per capita income in Latin America, the autobiography
of Malcolm X. We publish while others perish.

The gap between the products of scholarly activity and the needs
of a troubled world could be borne with some equanimity as long as
the nation seemed to be solving its problems. And for most of our history, this seemed to be the case. We had a race question, but we
"solved" it: by a war to end slavery, and by papering over the continued degradation of the black population with laws and rhetoric.
Wealth was not distributed equitably, but the New Deal, and then war
orders, kept that problem under control—or at least, out of sight.
There was turmoil in the world, but we were always at the periphery;
the European imperial powers did the nasty work, while we nibbled at
the edges of their empires (except in Latin America where our firm
control was disguised by a fatherly sounding Monroe Doctrine, and
the pose of a Good Neighbor).

None of those solutions is working anymore. The Black Power
revolt, the festering of cities beyond our control, the rebellion of students against the Vietnam war and the draft—all indicate that the
United States has run out of time, space, and rhetoric. The liberal arti-
facts that represented our farthest reaches toward reform—the

Fourteenth Amendment, New Deal welfare legislation, the U.N. Charter—are not enough. Revolutionary changes are required in social policy.

The trouble is, we don't know how to make such a revolution. There is no precedent for it in an advanced industrial society where power and wealth are highly concentrated in government, corporations, and the military, while the rest of us have pieces of that fragmented power political scientists are pleased to call "pluralism." We have voices, and even votes, but not the means—more crassly, the power—to turn either domestic or foreign policy in completely new directions.

That is why the knowledge industry (the universities, colleges, schools, representing directly $65 billion of the national spending each year) is so important. Knowledge is a form of power. True, force is the most direct form of power, and government has a monopoly on that (as Max Weber once pointed out). But in modern times, when social control rests on "the consent of the governed," force is kept in abeyance for emergencies, and everyday control is exercised by a set of rules, a fabric of values passed on from one generation to another by the priests and the teachers of the society. What we call the rise of democracy in the world means that force is replaced by deception (a blunt way of saying "education") as the chief method for keeping society as it is.

This makes knowledge important, because although it cannot confront force directly, it can counteract the deception that makes the government's force legitimate. And the knowledge industry, which directly reaches seven million young people in colleges and universities, thus becomes a vital and sensitive locus of power. That power can be used, as it was traditionally, to maintain the *status quo,* or (as is being demanded by the student rebels) to change it.

Those who command more obvious forms of power (political control and wealth) try also to commandeer knowledge. Industry entices some of the most agile minds for executive posts in business. Government lures others for more glamorous special jobs: physicists to work on H-bombs; biologists to work on what we might call, for want of a better name, the field of communicable disease; chemists to work on nerve gas (like that which killed 6,000 sheep in Utah); political scientists to work on counter-insurgency warfare; historians to sit in a room in the White House and wait for a phone call to let them know when history is being made, so they may record it. And sometimes one's field doesn't matter. War is interdisciplinary.

Most knowledge is not directly bought, however. It can also serve the purpose of social stability in another way—by being squandered on trivia. Thus, the university becomes a playpen in which the society invites its favored children to play—and gives them toys and prizes to keep them out of trouble. For instance, we might note an article in a leading journal of political science not long ago, dealing with the effects of *Hurricane Betsy* on the mayoralty election in New Orleans. Or, a team of social psychologists (armed with a fat government grant) may move right into the ghetto (surely the scholar is getting relevant here) and discover two important facts from its extensive, sophisticated research: that black people in the ghetto are poor, and that they have family difficulties.

I am touching a sensitive nerve in the academy now: am I trying to obliterate all scholarship except the immediately relevant? No, it is a matter of proportion. The erection of new skyscraper office buildings is not offensive in itself, but it becomes lamentable alongside the continued existence of ghetto slums. It was not wrong for the Association of Asian Studies at its last annual meeting to discuss some problems of the Ming Dynasty and a battery of similarly remote topics, but *no* session of the dozens at the meeting dealt with Vietnam.

Aside from trivial or esoteric inquiry, knowledge is also dissipated on pretentious conceptualizing in the social sciences. A catch phrase can become a stimulus for endless academic discussion, and for the proliferation of debates that go nowhere into the real world, only round and round in ever smaller circles of scholarly discourse. Schemes and models and systems are invented that have the air of profundity and that advance careers, but hardly anything else.

We should not be surprised then at the volatile demonstrations for black studies programs, or for the creation of new student-run courses based on radical critiques of American society. Students demanding relevance in scholarship have been joined by professors dissenting at the annual ceremonials called scholarly meetings: at the American Philosophical Association, a resolution denouncing U.S. policy in Vietnam; at the American Political Science Association, a new caucus making radical changes in the program; at the American Historical Association, a successful campaign removing the 1968 meeting from Chicago to protest Mayor Daley's hooliganism; at the Modern Language Association, the election of a young, radical English teacher as president.

Still we are troubled, because the new urgency to use our heads for good purposes gets tangled in a cluster of beliefs so stuck, fungus-like, to the scholar, that even the most activist of us cannot cleanly extricate ourselves. These beliefs are roughly expressed by the phrases "disinterested scholarship," "dispassionate learning," "objective study," "scientific method"—all adding up to the fear that using our intelligence to further our moral ends is somehow improper. And so we mostly remain subservient to the beliefs of the profession although they violate our deepest feelings as human beings, although we suspect that the traditional neutrality of the scholar is a disservice to the very ideals we teach about as history, and a betrayal of the victims of an unneutral world.

It may, therefore, be worthwhile to examine the arguments for "disinterested, neutral, scientific, objective" scholarship. If there is to be a revolution in the uses of knowledge to correspond to the revolution in society, it will have to begin by challenging the rules that sustain the wasting of knowledge. Let me cite a number of them, and argue briefly for new approaches.

Rule 1: *Carry on "disinterested scholarship."* (In one hour's reading some weeks ago I came across three such exhortations, using just that phrase: in an essay by Walter Lippmann; in the Columbia University Commencement Address of Richard Hofstadter; in an article by Daniel Bell, appearing, ironically in a magazine called *The Public Interest.*) The call is naive, because there are powerful interests already at work in the academy, with varying degrees of self-consciousness.

There is the Establishment of political power and corporate wealth, whose interest is that the universities produce people who will fit into existing niches in the social structure rather than try to change the structure. We always knew our educational system "socialized" people, but we never worried about this, because we assumed our social norms were worth perpetuating. Now, and rightly, we are beginning to doubt this. There is the interest of the educational bureaucracy in maintaining itself: its endowment, its buildings, its positions (both honorific and material), its steady growth along orthodox lines. These larger interests are internalized in the motivations of the scholar: promotion, tenure, higher salaries, prestige—all of which are best secured by innovating in prescribed directions.

All of these interests operate, not through any conspiratorial decision but through the mechanism of a well-oiled system, just as the irrationality of the economic system operates not through any devilish plot but through the mechanism of the profit motive and the market, and as the same kinds of political decisions reproduce themselves in Congress year after year.

No one *intends* exactly what happens. They just follow the normal rules of the game. Similarly with education; hence the need to challenge these rules that quietly lead the scholar toward trivia, pretentiousness, orotundity, and the production of objects: books, degrees, buildings, research projects, dead knowledge. (Emerson is still right: "*Things* are in the saddle, and ride mankind.")

There is no question then of a "disinterested" university, only a question about what kinds of interests the university will serve. There are fundamental humanistic interests—above any particular class, party, nation, ideology—that I believe the university should consciously serve. I assume this is what we mean when we speak (however we act) of fostering certain "values" in education.

The university should unashamedly declare that its interest is in eliminating war, poverty, race and national hatred, governmental restrictions on individual freedom, and in fostering a spirit of cooperation and concern in the generation growing up. It should *not* serve the interests of particular nations or parties or religions or political dogmas. Ironically, the university has often served narrow governmental, military, or business interests, and yet withheld support from larger, transcendental values, on the ground that it needed to maintain neutrality.

Rule 2: *Be objective.* The myth of "objectivity" in teaching and scholarship is based on a common confusion. If to be objective is to be scrupulously careful about reporting accurately what one sees, then of course this is laudable. But accuracy is only a prerequisite. Whether a metalsmith uses reliable measuring instruments is a prerequisite for doing good work, but does not answer the crucial question: will he now forge a sword or a plowshare with his instruments? That the metalsmith has determined in advance that he prefers a plowshare does not require him to distort his measurements. That the scholar has decided he prefers peace to war does not require him to distort his facts.

Too many scholars abjure a starting set of values, because they fail to make the proper distinction between an ultimate set of values and the instruments needed to obtain them. The values may well be subjective (derived from human needs); but the instruments must be objective (accurate). Our values should determine the questions we ask in scholarly inquiry, but not the answers.

Rule 3: *Stick to your discipline.* Specialization has become as absurdly extreme in the educational world as in the medical world. One no longer is a specialist in American government, but in Congress, or the Presidency, or pressure groups: a historian is a "colonialist" or an "early national period" man. This is natural when education is divorced from the promotion of values. To work on a real problem (such as how to eliminate poverty in a nation producing $800-billion worth of wealth each year), one would have to follow that problem across many disciplinary lines without qualm, dealing with historical materials, economic theories, political problems. Specialization insures that one cannot follow a problem through from start to finish. It ensures the functioning in the academy of the system's dictum: divide and rule.

Another kind of scholarly segregation serves to keep those in the university from dealing with urgent social problems: that which divorces fact from theory. We learn the ideas of the great philosophers and poets in one part of our educational experience. In the other part, we prepare to take our place in the real occupational world. In political science, for instance, a political theorist discusses transcendental visions of the good society; someone else presents factual descriptions of present governments. But no one deals with both the *is* and the *ought*; if they did, they would have to deal with how to get from here to there, from the present reality to the poetic vision. Note how little work is done in political science on the tactics of social change. Both student and teacher deal with theory and reality in separate courses; the compartmentalization safely neutralizes them.

It is time to recall Rousseau: "We have physicists, geometricians, chemists, astronomers, poets, musicians, and painters in plenty, but we have no longer a citizen among us."

Rule 4: *To be "scientific" requires neutrality.* This is a misconception of how science works, both in fact and in purpose. Scientists *do* have values, but they decided on these so long ago that we have forgotten them; they aim to save human life, to extend human control over the environment for the happiness of men and women. This is the tacit assumption behind scientific work, and a physiologist would be astonished if someone suggested that he starts from a neutral position as regards life or death, health or sickness. Somehow the social scientists have not yet got around to accepting openly that their aim is to keep people alive, to distribute equitably the resources of the earth, to widen the areas of human freedom, and therefore to direct their efforts toward these ends.

The claim that social science is "different," because its instruments are tainted with subjectivity, ignores the new discoveries in the hard sciences: that the very fact of observation distorts the measurement of the physicist, and what he sees depends on his position in space. The physical sciences do not talk about certainty anymore, but rather about "probability"; while the probabilities may be higher for them than in the social sciences, both fields are dealing with elusive data.

Rule 5: *A scholar must, in order to be "rational," avoid "emotionalism."* (I know one man in Asian studies who was told by university administrators that the articles he wrote upon his return from Vietnam were too "emotional.") True, emotion can distort. But it can also enhance. If one of the functions of the scholar is accurate description, then it is impossible to describe a war both unemotionally and accurately at the same time. And if the special competence of the mind is in enabling us to perceive what is outside our own limited experience, that competence is furthered, that perception sharpened, by emotion.

Even a large dose of emotionalism in the description of slavery would merely *begin* to convey accurately to a white college student what slavery was like for the black man.

Thus, exactly from the standpoint of what intellect is supposed to do for us—to extend the boundaries of our understanding—the "cool, rational, unemotional" approach fails. For too long, white Americans were emotionally separated from what the Negro suffered in this country by cold, and therefore inadequate, historical description. War and violence, divested of their brutality by the prosaic quality of the printed page, became tolerable to the young. (True, the poem and the novel were read in the English classes, but these were neatly separated from the history and government classes.) Reason, to be accurate, must be supplemented by emotion, as Reinhold Niebuhr once reminded us.

Refusing, then, to let ourselves be bound by traditional notions of disinterestedness, objectivity, scientific procedure, rationality—what kinds of work can scholars do, in deliberate unneutral pursuit of a more livable world? Am I urging Orwellian control of scholarly activities? Not at all. I am, rather suggesting that scholars, on their own, reconsider the rules by which they have worked, and begin to turn their intellectual energies to the urgent problems of our time.

Specifically, we might use our scholarly time and energy to sharpen the perceptions of the complacent by exposing those facts that any society tends to hide about itself: the facts about wealth and poverty, about tyranny in both communist and capitalist states, about lies told by politicians, the mass media, the church, popular leaders. We need to expose fallacious logic, spurious analogies, deceptive slogans, and those intoxicating symbols that drive people to murder (the flag, communism, capitalism, freedom). We need to dig beneath the abstractions so our fellow citizens can make judgments on the particular realities beneath political rhetoric. We need to expose inconsistencies and double standards. In short, we need to become the critics of the culture, rather than its apologists and perpetuators.

The university is especially gifted for such a task. Although obviously not remote from the pressures of business and military and politicians, it has just that margin of leeway, just that tradition of truth-telling (however violated in practice) that can enable it to become a spokesman for change.

This will require holding up before society forgotten visions, lost utopias, unfulfilled dreams—badly needed in this age of cynicism. Those outside the university who might act for change are deterred by pessimism. A bit of historical perspective, some recapitulation of the experience of social movements in other times, other places, while not wholly cheering, can at least suggest possibilities.

Along with inspirational visions, we will need specific schemes for accomplishing important purposes, which can then be laid before the groups that can use them. Let the economists work out a plan for free food, instead of advising the Federal Reserve Board on interest rates. Let the political scientists work out insurgency tactics for the poor, rather than counter-insurgency tactics for the military. Let the historians instruct us or inspire us, from the data of the past, rather than amusing us, boring us, or deceiving us. Let the scientists figure out and lay before the public plans on how to make autos safe, cities beautiful, air pure. Let all social scientists work on modes of change instead of merely describing the world that is, so that we can make the necessary revolutionary alterations with the least disorder.

I am not sure what a revolution in the academy will look like, any more than I know what a revolution in the society will look like. I doubt that it will take the form of some great cataclysmic event. More likely, it will be a process, with periods of tumult and of quiet, in which we will, here and there, by ones and twos and tens, create pockets of concern inside old institutions, transforming them from within.

There is no great day of reckoning to work toward. Rather, we must begin *now* to liberate those patches of ground on which we stand—to "vote" for a new world (as Thoreau suggested) with our whole selves all the time, rather than in moments carefully selected by others.

Thus, we will be acting out the beliefs that always moved us as humans but rarely as scholars. To do that, we will need to defy the professional mythology that has kept us on the tracks of custom, our eyes averted (except for moments of charity) from the cruelty on all sides. We will be taking seriously for the first time the words of the great poets and philosophers whom we love to quote but not to emulate. We will be doing this, not in the interest of the rich and powerful, or in behalf of our own careers, but for those who have never had a chance to read poetry or study philosophy, who so far have had to strive alone just to stay warm in winter, to stay alive through the calls for war.

21

Freedom Schools

One of the remarkable achievements of the 1964 Mississippi Summer, when people came from all over the country to work with the civil rights movement, was the Freedom School. Thirty years later, it still stands, I think, as an extraordinary experiment in educational democracy. My wife Roslyn and I were in Mississippi that summer, and I volunteered to teach in one of the Freedom Schools in Jackson. I wrote this account for *The Nation*, November 23, 1964. It appeared under the title "Schools in Context: The Mississippi Idea."

The triple murder last summer in Mississippi probably would not have taken place if there had not been plans to set up a school at the Mount Zion Baptist Church near Philadelphia. It was the visit of three young civil rights workers to the burned-out school site which led them to arrest, and then death. That a school should frighten a band of Americans into committing murder is not totally credible; that those particular killers made a deliberate mental connection between their act and the establishment of a "Freedom School" in the area is unlikely. Yet education spells danger to certain people at certain times, and what happened in Mississippi last summer suggests a continued sensing of peril.

This article will be concerned, however, not so much with the danger the Freedom Schools represented to some in Mississippi but with the promise they opened for the rest of us, throughout America. For eight weeks, more than 2,000 Negro youngsters, averaging fifteen years of age but ranging from six to twenty-six and older, went to schools which violated all the rules and regulations of educational orthodoxy. They were taught by teachers who met no official qualifications; they assembled in church basements or on the streets or in the fields; they came and went without attendance records, grades or examinations.

It was an experiment that cannot be assessed in the usual terms of "success" and "failure," and it would be wrong to hail it with an enthusiasm which would then lead it to be judged by traditional criteria. But that venture of last summer in Mississippi deserves close attention by all Americans interested in the relationship between education and social change.

The idea, and the term "freedom school," were first brought before the civil rights movement by a slender Howard University student named Charles Cobb, who several years ago interrupted his studies to plunge into the Mississippi Delta as a field secretary for the Student Nonviolent Coordinating Committee. Cobb pursued his scheme with quiet, slow persistence, and when plans were laid last fall for a big "Mississippi Summer," with 1,000 or more volunteers to arrive in the state, Freedom Schools were on the agenda. Bob Moses, director of the Mississippi project, has a Masters degree from Harvard. He gave the idea close attention, and when Northern students were recruited during the spring many of them were told to be ready to teach.

The man who took charge of the summer Freedom School project for COFO (the Council of Federated Organizations: a union of SNCC, CORE and other civil rights groups in Mississippi) was

Staughton Lynd, a young historian whose field, some might have noted warningly, is the American Revolution. He had spent three years in north Georgia in a rural cooperative community, and then three more years at Spelman College, a Negro women's college in Atlanta. He had just resigned from Spelman in protest against restrictions on the academic freedom of both students and faculty, and was then immediately hired by Yale University. From the orientation session at Oxford, Ohio, in early June to the end of August, Lynd was a dynamo of an administrator, driving into the remotest rural regions of Mississippi to keep the schools going.

At Oxford, the Freedom School teachers were warned about difficulties: "You'll arrive in Ruleville, in the Delta. It will be 100 degrees, and you'll be sweaty and dirty. You won't be able to bathe often or sleep well or eat good food. The first day of school, there may be four teachers and three students. And the local Negro minister will phone to say you can't use his church basement after all, because his life has been threatened. And the curriculum we've drawn up—Negro history and American government—may be something you know only a little about yourself. Well, you'll knock on doors all day in the hot sun to find students. You'll meet on someone's lawn under a tree. You'll tear up the curriculum and teach what you know."

They were also told to be prepared for violence, injury, even death. But they hardly expected it so soon. The first batch of teachers had just left the orientation session for Mississippi when word came that one of the summer volunteers (Andrew Goodman), a white community center director (Mickey Schwerner) and a local Meridian Negro youth (James Chaney) were missing. A publicity stunt, said Mississippi officials. But the SNCC veterans of Mississippi disagreed. "Man, those guys are dead," Jim Forman said.

The summer volunteers got into cars and into buses, and moved into Mississippi. Two hundred Freedom School teachers spread out over the state, from Biloxi in the Gulf Coast up into Ruleville in the Delta, and farther north to Holly Springs, covering twenty-five communities. Day by day, more and more Negro kids came around to the schools, and the expected enrollment of 1,000 rose to 1,500 then to 2,000.

One of the Jackson Freedom Schools opened in early August in a church basement just a short walk from the state COFO office on Lynch Street. Its combination of disorder and inspiration was very much like that of the other schools in the state. The "faculty" was more experienced than most: a young high school teacher of English from Vermont acted as "coordinator"—a combination of principal, janitor, recreation supervisor, and father confessor. Another youthful junior high school teacher of mathematics was from Brooklyn; there was one college professor of history who had taught for a number of years in a Southern Negro college; also, an enthusiastic young woman named Jimmy Miller, whose husband, Warren Miller, had written in *The Cool World* about young Harlem Negro kids. The teachers lived in spare rooms, or spare corners of rooms, in Negro houses of the neighborhood.

Two days before the school was set to open, in close to 100 degree heat, the teachers canvassed the neighborhood for students. Each asked one of the Negro youngsters hanging around the COFO office to go along with him, so as to establish from the start that these were friendly visitors walking up on the porches, knocking on the doors, asking: "Do y'all know about the Freedom School starting on Wednesday over at Pratt Memorial Church?" No, they mostly didn't, and so the information passed across the threshold: "It's for teen-age boys and girls, to learn about Negro history, and the Constitution, and the civil rights movement, and mathematics, and maybe French and Spanish, the way they don't get learning in the regular school." Kids on bicycles stopped, and one friend told another, and the word was passed on.

No one paid attention to details like age requirements, so that at the opening of school, sixty kids showed up, from six to nineteen;

Jimmy Miller marched the six to ten children off to a corner, to read with them, and teach them freedom songs, and sound out French words whose English equivalents they had not yet discovered, and painstakingly correct their spelling.

With the older ones, fourteen to nineteen, any idea of going in an organized way through an outline of Negro history or American government was soon dropped. Beyond a core of seven or eight who came faithfully every morning at nine and stayed until mid-afternoon, there were a dozen others who came and went as they liked. So the history professor started each day from where the mood struck him, from some point on which he thought the students' recognition might be fastened just long enough to pull them onward.

One day, it was an editorial in the morning's *Clarion-Ledger*, charging that civil rights workers were teaching people to break the law. "What do you think about that editorial? Is it true? If you could write a letter to the editor about it, what would you say?...Here's paper and pencil, go ahead. We'll pick out one or two and *really* send them to the editor." This was not education for grades, not writing for teacher's approval, but for an immediate use; it was a learning surrounded with urgency. And the students responded with seriousness, picking apart the issues: Are we for the law? Is there a higher law? When is civil disobedience justified? Then the teacher explored with them the differences between statutory law, constitutional law, "natural" law.

On another day the teacher told his students about the annual fair he had visited the previous afternoon. It was held in Neshoba County where the bodies of the three murdered civil rights workers had just been discovered. A strain of tension and fear pervaded the crowds that day at the fair. Gov. Paul Johnson had said: "It is not Mississippi's obligation to enforce federal statutes." A representative of the John Birch Society had said: "I am for the Constitution, for freedom, for the open Bible." The students were asked: Do you disagree? Aren't you for the

Constitution? For freedom? The discussion became heated. Distinctions were drawn, and became more and more refined, all by the students themselves, the teacher just listening: "Which Constitution does he mean, U.S. or Mississippi?...Maybe we're for different *parts* of the U.S. Constitution...Well, maybe we're for the same part, but we *interpret* it differently."

Teachers and students ate lunch together in the church basement, sang together, then separated into various activities. In a creative writing class, a teen-age girl named Lillie Mae Powell wrote a poem "The Negro Soldier":

> One day while I was visiting a certain
> City this is what I saw. A Negro
> soldier with a broken arm who
> was wounded in the war.
>
> The wind was blowing from the
> North; there was a drizzle of
> Rain. He was looking from the
> Last place; his arm was in a sling.
>
> The Negro soldier didn't go
> Home. He was looking to the east
> And to the west. His broken arm
> was in a sling.

The Jackson Freedom Schools faced only mild harassment. Early in the session, while canvassing for more students, two teachers—one a slim, blonde Skidmore undergraduate—were picked up by the police, held for several hours, then discharged. Violence spluttered around the COFO office in Jackson one ugly Saturday night: a young man building book shelves for a Freedom School bookmobile on the street across from the office was clubbed to the ground by a white man who fled in a car; a dance hall where teachers and students were spending the evening was sprayed with bullets by a passing car, and a Negro boy was wounded; crosses were burned. But by Mississippi standards, Jackson was peaceful.

In the rural areas of the state, the danger was greater. A church used as a Freedom School in the little town of Fluckstadt was burned to the ground (when the teachers arrived on the scene, fifteen youngsters were waiting under a tree for class to begin). A Northern doctor who spent the summer in Mississippi with the movement told of the two white girls who lived along in a hilltop house out in the country, 30 miles from Canton, and held a Freedom School there. In McComb, so dangerous that the Justice Department pleaded with the Mississippi project not to send anyone in there, a Freedom School was started by a Washington, D.C., speech teacher, a young Negro named Ralph Featherstone. Two days after the first contingent arrived, a bomb exploded in the midst of sleeping SNCC workers. But 100 children came regularly to attend the McComb Freedom School.

Violence took the headlines, but behind it a phenomenal thing was happening to Mississippi: 2,000 young people were having experiences that would—for some in a small way, for some drastically—change their lives.

The kind of teaching that was done in the Freedom Schools was, despite its departure from orthodoxy—or, more likely, because of it—just about the best kind there is. For the teachers were selected not by any mechanical set of requirements but on the basis of general intelligence, enthusiasm and the kind of social conscience that would drive them to spend a hot summer in Mississippi without pay. They taught, not out of textbooks, but out of life, trying to link the daily headlines with the best and deepest of man's intellectual tradition.

Their object was not to cram a prescribed amount of factual material into young minds, but to give them that first look into new worlds which would, some day if not immediately, lead them to books and people and ideas not found in the everyday lives of Mississippi

Negroes. They didn't always succeed, but even their failures were warmed by the affection that sprang up everywhere between teachers and students, both aware that they talked with one another inside a common cradle of concern.

One afternoon in Jackson, a visiting folk singer brought the students of a Freedom School out into the sun-baked street back of the church, formed them into a huge circle, and taught them an Israeli dance chant imploring the heavens for rain to help the harvest. Older Negroes passed by, sat on porches, listened to their children utter strange words and dance this strange dance. The young ones seemed to understand; they were beginning, for the first time in their lives, to reach beyond their street, beyond their state, to join in some universal plea.

A Stanford University professor of English told how hard he had to work to make contact with these young boys and girls, so different from his regular students. But it came. He walked into class, put them at ease with some foolery, got them to talk about the events in the morning newspaper. Then: "Who would like to read a story?" One girl stubbornly had her back to the class. He asked her to read and she turned around. "She then read this story by Eudora Welty, 'The Worn Path,' and read it beautifully; it could have been a staged performance. And this was back of the church, the only place we had for my class, with the noise of traffic all around."

When the girl finished reading, the teacher asked the class: "Did you like the story?" There was a chorus: "Yes!" "Why?" They responded. He told them about subject and plot, about description and dialogue, how in general one analyzes a story. He asked how the story made them *feel*, and one said sad, and another said it made her laugh, and he asked how could a story do both at the same time, and spoke to them of *irony*. "God, how they understood!"

He bridged what they read and how they lived. He read to them from Ralph Ellison's *Invisible Man*. This was written, he said out of a

Negro boy's personal experience. "Now I'll tell you a story of my personal experience." And he told of a wartime incident involving himself and Negro soldiers, in Charleston, South Carolina. And then, to the class: "Who else wants to tell a personal story?" The next day, one girl brought in a story which, he realized, was prose as good as that written by any Stanford freshmen he had encountered. And so, literature was read and created at the same time.

In these classes, discussions of democracy, of the philosophy of nonviolence, were hardly academic. In one Jackson school the class met to elect delegates to a convention of all the Jackson Freedom Schools. An older fellow named Jimmy, age 24, had been hanging around the class for the past few days. He spoke breezily of having recently spent three years in jail for a knifing. The teacher suggested that Jimmy sit up at the desk and chair the meeting. He laughed and complied, "OK, now, I'll choose the delegates," he announced. There were objections from all over the room: "We've got to *elect* them"!

"What kind of resolutions are we going to propose to the convention?" a girl asked. One was suggested: "If any kid is treated brutally in school in Jackson, all the kids in the Jackson schools walk out; we'll have a chairman in each school; we won't act just on say-so; we'll get written affidavits and witnesses before we take action. It's something like a student union."

The teacher was curious: "Do students get beaten up in your schools?" A girl answered: her principal had beaten a boy until he bled.

Jimmy then told how he'd been beaten by a teacher when he was younger. And how he and some friends had then found the teacher alone and taken revenge. "We had a nice understanding after that." He hesitated. "But I don't know what I'd do now. You know this nonviolence we're talking about. If it happened now I might beat him. Or I might just laugh and go away. I was young then and full of hate. At that time, I see something I want. I take it. Now, I *ask*. It's the movement I guess...I want my son to come up different."

Role playing was used very often in the Freedom Schools. "Kids that age are natural actors," a teacher explained. "And it puts them in other people's shoes. We don't want to win easy arguments over straw foes. They have got to be tough thinkers, tough arguers." The teacher listed on the blackboard Barry Goldwater's reasons for voting against the civil rights bill: (1) It is unconstitutional. (2) No law will end prejudice ("We cannot pass a law that will make you like me or me like you."). (3) It can't be enforced. (4) It violates the idea of States' rights. The class went over the arguments, with one boy portraying Goldwater, and defending his points powerfully, another trying to break them down.

Outside on the street, in front of the building, an energetic, red-headed teacher was pointing to a blackboard propped up in the sun, the kids sitting in rows in the shade of the building. "OK, we can build any kind of community we want now. What will the rules be?" This was a hortatory kind of teaching, but a kind the schools fostered: constantly talking with students not just about what *is*, but about what *should be*.

A Harvard graduate in literature who had taught in Israel worked in a Vicksburg Freedom School.

> It was hard. Youngsters hung around the school, slept there. Every morning, they were like corpses on the floor. To start class, you had to clean them out. The school was cramped, noisy. We used role playing a lot. Kids would portray three generations of Negro families, and we learned history that way. We sat in a circle rather than the usual classroom format, to stress the equality of teacher and student. I read to them from Thomas Wolfe's *You Can't Go Home Again* and from Martin Luther King's *I Have a Dream*, then had them write speeches as if they were Senators urging passage of the civil rights bill. I tried to extend the idea of oppression beyond race. If you pick on a small kid with glasses and beat him up, aren't you acting the same as these white segregationists? I asked them.

One teacher spent a whole hour with his students discussing the word "skeptical." He told them: "This is a Freedom School and we should mean what we say. We should feel free to think as we want, question whomever we like, whether it's our parents, our ministers, our teachers, yes, me, right here. Don't take my word for things. Check up on them. Be *skeptical*." For these youngsters it was a new way of looking at the classroom. They told how in their high school in Jackson the rooms were wired so that at the flick of a switch the principal could listen in on any class in the school. Teachers were afraid to discuss controversial subjects.

The blonde girl from Skidmore College taught French to teen-agers in her Freedom School. "I try to do the whole class in French, use pantomime a lot...I soon realized these kids had never had contact with a white person before; maybe that's the greatest thing about this whole experience. If nothing else is accomplished, it's been a *meeting*, for both student and teacher.... We have a Freedom Hour at eleven every morning. They run it themselves, make their own rules." She was asked if the Freedom Schools were not, in fact, *indoctrinating* the children. She paused. "Yes, I suppose so. But I can't think of anything better to indoctrinate them with. Freedom. Justice. The Golden Rule. Isn't there *some* core of belief a school should stand by?"

A green-eyed, attractive Radcliffe graduate, interpreter now for an international agency, whose field was Latin American history but who had not a day of teaching experience or education courses to her cred-it, went to work in a Freedom School:

> My kids were 9 to 13. I told them about the Spanish background of Negro slaves in the United States, about the Caribbean islands and the slave plan-tation system as it developed there, and compared that system with the one in the English colonies. I spoke to them about life in Brazil, about the mul-tiracial societies in Latin America where people get along fine. I told them

about the problems of kids their age in Venezuela, in Puerto Rico (where I've spent some time). Yes, it did something for them psychologically to know that there are people in the world worse off than they are!

Without a strict curriculum to follow, the schools capitalized on the unexpected. A class held out in the sun would take advantage of passers-by, draw them into discussion. One day, three Negro women came by who'd just been trying to register to vote and had been rebuffed. The teacher beckoned: "Come over here and tell my students what happened." And so the children learned about the registration procedure, about voting, about what to tell their parents about going down to register. One of the middle-aged women, her anger still fresh, told them they must become educated if they wanted to change things.

It was risky, teaching without an ordered curriculum. And because it was risky, the Radcliffe girl said, it led to treasures.

> I could experiment, do what I wanted, try things completely new, because I had no one to answer to, no reports to make. Nothing could happen to me or to these young people that would leave us worse off than before. And I could go off on tangents whenever I wanted, something I'd be afraid to do in a regular school setup. Wherever thoughts and discussion led, we followed. There was nothing we didn't dare turn to.

The road from study to action was short. Those who attended the schools began to come to mass rallies, to canvass for registration of voters, to question things around them for the first time. In Shaw County, "out in the rural," when the regular school began its session in August (Negro schools in the Delta open in August so that the children will be available for cotton picking in the fall), white Freedom School teachers were turned away from the regular school cafeteria, where some students had invited them to a lunch. The students then boycotted the school and flocked in large numbers to the local Freedom School.

The Freedom Schools' challenge to the social structure of Mississippi was obvious from the start. Its challenge to American education as a whole is more subtle. There is, to begin with, the provocative suggestion that an entire school system can be created in any community outside the official order, and critical of its suppositions. But beyond that, other questions were posed by the Mississippi experiment of last summer.

Can we, somehow, bring teachers and students together, not through the artificial sieve of certification and examination but on the basis of their common attraction to an exciting social goal? Can we solve the old educational problem of teaching children crucial values, while avoiding a blanket imposition of the teacher's ideas? Can this be done by honestly accepting as an educational goal that we want better human beings in the rising generation than we had in the last, and that this requires a forthright declaration that the educational process cherishes equality, justice, compassion and world brotherhood? Is it not possible to create a hunger for those goals through the fiercest argument about whether or not they *are* worthwhile? And cannot the schools have a running, no-ideas-barred exchange of views about alternative ways to those goals?

Is there, in the floating, prosperous, nervous American social order of the Sixties, a national equivalent to the excitement of the civil rights movement, one strong enough in its pull to create a motivation for learning that even the enticements of monetary success cannot match? Would it be possible to declare boldly that the aim of the schools is to find solutions for poverty, for injustice, for race and national hatred, and to turn all educational efforts into a national striving for those solutions?

Perhaps people can begin, here and there (not waiting for the government, but leading it) to set up other pilot ventures, imperfect but suggestive, like the one last summer in Mississippi. Education can, and should, be dangerous.

22

Historian as Citizen

This piece appeared as an essay in the Sunday book review section of *The New York Times*, September 25, 1966. Although I had been educated in a very traditional way at New York University and Columbia University, and done a year of postdoctoral work at Harvard University, I had not been behaving like a traditional historian. That is, I had taken time out of scholarly work to participate in the Southern movement for civil rights, and, now living in Boston and teaching at Boston University, I was heavily involved in the movement against the war in Vietnam. This essay gave me an opportunity to think about the relationship between my two lives, as historian, as activist, and to turn from simply practicing what I called "history as private enterprise," to history as the work of a citizen.

When some historians march with Negroes in the South, and others demonstrate against Presidential foreign policy, one is led to wonder if we are witnessing a slow change in role for the historian. Traditionally, he is a passive observer, one who looks for sequential patterns in the past as a guide to the future, or else describes historical events as unique and disorderly—but without participating himself in attempts to change the pattern or tidy the disorder.

In a world hungry for solutions, we ought to welcome the emergence of the historian—if this is really what we are seeing—as an activist-scholar, who thrusts himself and his works into the crazy mechanism of history, on behalf of values in which he deeply believes. This makes of him more than a scholar; it makes him a citizen in the ancient Athenian sense of the word.

The historian is one man among men, and how free is any man to change the world in which he lives? The world's great thinkers have been quite aware of the paradox of man as both created and creative, and acted accordingly. But thinking has become professionalized and "disciplined" in modern times, with a crushing effect on the propensity to act.

For historians, there is an additional trap: The more we work on the data of the past, the weightier the past seems. Events that have already taken place develop the look of having been *necessary;* indeed they were, but only at the instant they occurred, when further interference was impossible. This necessariness of the past tends to infect our thinking about the future, weighing down our disposition to act. Man is wounded by his history, and we then assume he must be transfixed by it.

History can work another way, however. If the present seems an irrevocable fact of nature, the past is most usable as a way of suggesting possibilities we would never otherwise consider; it can both warn and inspire. By probing the past we can counter myths which affect the way we act today. We can see that it is possible for an entire nation to be brainwashed; for an "advanced, educated" people to commit genocide; for a "progressive, democratic" nation to maintain slavery; for apparently powerless subordinates to defeat their rulers; for economic planning to be unaccompanied by restrictions on freedom; for oppressed to turn into oppressors; for "socialism" to be tyrannical; for a whole people to be led to war like sheep; for men to make incredible sacrifices on behalf of a cause.

Yet the historical experience of mankind does have limits; while it suggests some of the things that are possible, it has not at all exhausted the possibilities. Bounded in our imaginations, tyrannized by the past, we do not realize there is a universe of tricks still to be played. The past, in other words, suggests what can be, not what must be.

This is not at all to say that we are completely free at any moment in time. There is a remorselessly factual world which assails us at every turn, every decision. But because this world is *here* it exerts a disproportionate influence on our actions. The only way to compensate for this is to behave *as if* we are freer than we think. We can never—because the present is harsh and the future is shadow—weigh accurately how free we are, what our possibilities are at any moment. With such uncertainty, and recognizing the tendency toward overestimating the present, there is good reason for acting on the supposition of freedom.

Erik Erikson speaks in *Insight and Responsibility* about psychologists surprised by the strength of people, which seems to come, he says, from "unexpected encounters...and from opportunities beyond our theoretical anticipations."

Acting *as if* is a way of resolving the paradox of determinism and freedom, a way of overcoming the tension between past and future. It is risky to act as if we are free, but (unless one is content with things as they are) it is just as risky to act as if we are bound, and there is even less chance of reward. The leaps that man has made in social evolution came from those who acted *as if;* the four Negro youngsters in Greensboro who in 1960 walked into Woolworth's acted as if they would be served; Garrison and Phillips, against all apparent common sense, acted as if they would arouse a cold nation against slavery;

England in 1940 acted as if it could repel a German invasion; Castro and his tiny group in the hills behaved as if they could take over Cuba.

Nietzsche in *The Use and Abuse of History* attacked the bullying nature of history and the sterility of academic historiography. His opening words were quoted from Goethe: "I hate everything that merely instructs me without increasing or directly quickening my activity." He called the formal detached-from-life history of his time "a costly and superfluous luxury of the understanding" while people "are still in want of the necessaries of life."

Later in this same essay, Nietzsche calls for man to free himself from the past. "People think nothing but this troublesome reality of ours is possible." And at another point he speaks of the "historically educated fanatic of the world-process" who "has nothing to do but to live on as he has lived, love what he has loved, hate what he has hated, and read the newspapers he has always read. The only sin is for him to live otherwise than he has lived."

This is the Existentialist call for Freedom, for Action, for the exercise of Responsibility by man. Too often these days the Existentialists are accused of a blind refusal to recognize the limits set by the world around them. Sartre, trying to reconcile Existentialism and Marxism, is attempting the impossible, critics have said. But Sartre does not fail to see the armies, the prisons, the blind judges, the deaf rulers, the passive masses. He talks the language of total Freedom because he knows that acting *as if* we are free is the only way to break the bind.

To see our responsibility to present and future, is a radically different approach to history, for the traditional concern of academic history, from the start of investigation to the finish, is with the past, with only a few words muttered from time to time to indicate that all this digging in the archives "will help to understand the present." This encirclement of the historian by the past has an ironic effect in the making of moral judgments.

The usual division among historians is between those who declare, as Herbert Butterfield does in *History and Human Relations*, that the historian must avoid moral judgments, and those, like Geoffrey Barraclough in *History in a Changing World*, who deplore the loss of moral absolutes in a wave of "historicism" and "relativism." What is ironic is the fact that when historians do make moral judgments they are *about the past*, and in a way that may actually weaken moral responsibility in the present.

Moral indignation over Nazism illustrates the point. When such judgment becomes focused on an individual, it buries itself with that person and sticks to no one else. It follows that Germans who obeyed orders during the war may now weep at a showing of *The Diary of Anne Frank*, blaming the whole thing on Adolf Hitler. (How often these days in Germany does one hear "if not for Adolf Hitler..."?) It is this *ad hominem* assignment of responsibility, this searching the wrong place for blame with a kind of moral astigmatism, which Hannah Arendt tried to call attention to in her dissection of the Eichmann case.

But is it any better to widen responsibility from the individual to the group? Suppose we blame "the Nazis." Now that the Nazi party is disbanded, now that anti-Semitism is once again diffuse, now that militarism is the property of the "democratic" Government of West Germany as well as the "socialist" Government of East Germany, doesn't that kind of specific attribution of blame merely deflect attention from the problems of today? If we widen it so as to include Germans and Germany, what effect does this have except to infinitesimally decrease the sale of Volkswagens, and to permit every other nation in the world but Germany to commit mayhem in a softer glow?

What we normally do then, in making moral judgments, is assign responsibility to a group which in some specific historic instance was guilty, instead of selecting the elements of wrong, out of time and place (except for dramatic effect), so that they can be applicable to everyone including ourselves. (Is this not why Brecht, Kafka, Orwell are so powerful?)

It is racism, nationalism, militarism (among other elements) which we find reprehensible in Nazism. To put it that way is alarming, because those elements are discoverable not just in the past, but now, and not just in Germany, but in all the great powers, including the United States.

I am suggesting that blame in history be based on the future and not the past. It is an old and useless game among historians to decide whether Caesar was good or bad. Napoleon progressive or reactionary, Roosevelt a reformer or a revolutionist. True, certain of these questions are pertinent to present concerns; for instance, was Socrates right in submitting to Athens? But in a recounting of past crimes, the proper question to ask is not "Who was guilty then?" unless it leads directly to: "What is our responsibility now?"

Erikson, in a section of his *Insight and Responsibility* entitled "Psychological Reality and Historical Actuality," speaks of Freud's concern because this patient Dora had confronted her family with some of their misdeeds. "Freud considered this forced confrontation an act of revenge not compatible with the kind of insight which he had tried to convey to the patient. If she now knew that those events had caused her to fall ill, it was her responsibility to gain health, not revenge, from her insight." What makes this story even more interesting is that there is a suggestion that Freud may himself have been guilty of the same thing, by being annoyed with what his patient had done, and discontinuing her treatment.

It is this irony in moral judgment which explains why we are surprised when someone like George Kennan opposes a "moralistic" approach to other countries. This approach, he says—correctly—looks backward rather than forward. It leads to fixed enmities and fixed friendships, both based on past conditions; it prohibits a flexibility in the future.

In politics, the practice is common to all sides. When the Soviet Union defines imperialism as a characteristic of capitalist nations, it is limiting the ability of its people to criticize undue influence exerted over another country by a socialist nation. When it defines corruption as a manifestation of "bourgeois" culture, it makes it more difficult to deal with such a phenomenon in its own society. When the United States defines the Soviet sphere as "totalitarian" and the West as "free," it becomes difficult for Americans to see totalitarian elements in our society, and liberal elements in Soviet society. Moralizing in this way, we can condemn the Russians in Hungary and absolve ourselves in Vietnam.

To *define* an evil in terms of a specific group when such an evil is not peculiar to that group but possible anywhere is to remove responsibility from ourselves. It is what we have always done in criminal law, which is based on revenge for past acts, rather than a desire to make constructive social changes. (Capital punishment notably, but also all imprisonment, illustrates this.) It is often said that the French are always prepared for the previous war. In the modern world, we are always ready to identify those responsible for the previous act of evil.

Both history and art should instruct us. The crucial thing is to reveal the relationship between evil and ourselves. This makes it enormously useful to show how Hitler could emerge out of a boy playing in the field. Or to show (as in *Lord of the Flies*) how innocent children can become monsters, or (as in Bergman's film *The Virgin Spring*) how a loving father can become a vengeful murderer or (as in *Who's Afraid of Virginia Woolf?*) how an "ordinary" man and wife can become vultures.

But to survey the atrocities in world history and to conclude (as the defense lawyer did in the film *Judgment at Nuremberg*) that "we are all guilty" leads us nowhere when it neglects to identify the elements of failure so that we can recognize them in the future. On the other hand, to end by punishing the specific persons who were indeed guilty is to leave us all free to act, unnoticed, in the same way. For when our day of judgment comes, it will be, like all the others, one disaster late.

If a work like *The Deputy* succeeds in having people ask not Why did the Pope remain silent? but, Why do people everywhere, at all times, and *now*, remain silent? then the play itself has broken the silence of the stage. And those of us who are deputies of that Muse, History, now need to break ours.

PART 6

Portraits

23

Eugene Debs and the Idea of Socialism

When the Soviet Union disintegrated in 1989, we heard a constant refrain in the press and from the mouths of politicians, that socialism had been discredited, and capitalism was the wave of the future. I was annoyed by the way Stalinism was mistaken for socialism, and wanted to recapture that idea of socialism which had inspired millions of people in this country before the Bolshevik revolution ever existed. No one represented that idea more eloquently than the socialist leader Eugene Debs.

We are always in need of radicals who are also lovable and so we would do well to bring back to public attention the person of Eugene Victor Debs. Ninety years ago, at the time *The Progressive* was born, Debs was nationally famous as leader of the Socialist Party, and the poet James Whitcomb Riley wrote of him:

As warm a heart as ever beat
Betwixt here and the Judgement Seat

Debs was what every socialist or anarchist or radical should be: fierce in his convictions, kind and compassionate in his personal relations. Sam Moore, a fellow inmate of the Atlanta penitentiary, where Debs was imprisoned for opposing the first world war, told, years later, how he felt as Debs was about to be released on Christmas Day, 1921: "As miserable as I was, I would defy fate with all its cruelty as long as Debs held my hand, and I was the most miserably happiest man on earth when I knew he was going home Christmas."

Debs had won the hearts of his fellow prisoners in Atlanta. He had fought for them in a hundred ways, and refused any special privileges for himself. That day of Debs' release from Atlanta prison, the warden ignored prison regulations and opened every cellblock to allow over two thousand inmates to mass in front of the main jail building to say goodbye to Eugene Debs. As he started down the walkway from the prison, a roar went up and he turned, tears streaming down his face, and stretched out his arms to the other prisoners.

This was not his first prison experience. In 1894, not yet a Socialist, but an organizer of railroad workers in the American Railway Union, he had led a nationwide boycott of the railroads in support of the striking workers at the Pullman Palace Car Company. They effectively tied up the railroad system, burned hundreds of railway cars, and were met with the full force of the capitalist state: Attorney General Richard Olney, a former railroad lawyer, got a court injunction to prohibit blocking trains. President Cleveland called out the army, which used bayonets, and rifle fire on a crowd of five thousand strike sympathizers in Chicago. Seven hundred were arrested. Thirteen were shot to death.

Debs was jailed for violating a court injunction prohibiting him from doing or saying anything to carry on the strike. In court, he denied he was a socialist, but during his six months in prison he read socialist literature, and the events of the strike took on a deeper meaning. He wrote later: "I was to be baptized in Socialism in the roar of conflict...in the gleam of every bayonet and the flash of every rifle the class struggle was revealed...."

From then on Debs devoted his life energy to the cause of working people, and the dream of a socialist society. He stood on the platform with Mother Jones and Big Bill Haywood in 1905 at the founding convention of the Industrial Workers of the World. He was a magnificent speaker, his long body leaning forward from the podium, his arm raised dramatically. Thousands came to hear him talk, all over the country.

With the outbreak of war in Europe in 1914, and the build-up of war fever against Germany, some Socialists succumbed to the talk of "preparedness," but Debs was adamantly opposed. When President Wilson and Congress brought the nation into the war in 1917, speech was no longer free. The Espionage Act made it a crime to say anything that would discourage enlistment in the armed forces.

Soon, close to a thousand people were in prison for protesting the war. The producer of a movie called *The Spirit of '76,* about the American revolution, was sentenced to ten years in prison for promoting anti-British feeling at a time when England and the U.S. were allies, and thus discouraging enlistment in the military. The case was officially labeled *The U.S. vs. 'The Spirit Of '76.'*

Debs made a speech in Canton, Ohio in support of the men and women in jail for opposing the war. He told his listeners: "Wars throughout history have been waged for conquest and plunder.... And that is war in a nutshell. The master class has always declared the wars; the subject class has always fought the battles." He was found guilty, and sentenced to ten years in prison by a judge who denounced those "who would strike the sword from the hand of this nation while she is engaged in defending herself against a foreign and brutal power."

In court, Debs had refused to call any witnesses, declaring: "I have been accused of obstructing the war. I admit it. I abhor war. I would oppose war if I stood alone." Before sentencing, Debs spoke to judge and jury, uttering perhaps his most famous words (in his home town of Terre Haute, Indiana, recently, I was among two hundred people gathered to honor Debs' memory, who began the evening by reciting those words, words which moved me deeply when I first read them): "While there is a lower class, I am in it. While there is a criminal element, I am of it. While there is a soul in prison, I am not free."

The "liberal" Oliver Wendell Holmes, speaking for a unanimous Supreme Court, upheld the verdict, on the ground that Debs' speech was intended to obstruct military recruiting. The "liberal" Woodrow Wilson, with the war over, and Debs still in prison, sixty-five, and in poor health, turned down his Attorney General's recommendation that Debs be released. He was in prison for thirty two months, and then in 1921, the Republican Warren Harding ordered him freed on Christmas Day.

Today, when capitalism, "the free market," "private enterprise," are being hailed as triumphant in the world, as the system to be exported to every part of the world, it is a good time to remember Debs, and to rekindle, the idea of socialism.

To see the disintegration of the Soviet Union as a sign of the failure of socialism, is to mistake the monstrous tyranny created by Stalin for the vision of an egalitarian and democratic society which has inspired enormous numbers of people all over the world. Indeed, the removal of the Soviet Union as the false surrogate for the idea of socialism creates a great opportunity. We can now reintroduce genuine socialism to a world feeling the sickness of capitalism—its nationalist hatreds, its perpetual warfare, riches for a small number of people in a small number of countries, and hunger, homelessness, insecurity for everyone else.

Here in the United States we should recall that enthusiasm for socialism—production for use instead of profit, economic and social equality, solidarity with our brothers and sisters all over the world— was at its height before the Soviet Union came into being.

In the era of Debs, the first seventeen years of the twentieth century—until war created an opportunity to crush the movement—millions of Americans declared their adherence to the principles of socialism. Those were years of bitter labor struggles, the great walkouts of women garment workers in New York, the victorious multi-ethnic strike of textile workers in Lawrence, Massachusetts, the unbelievable courage of coal miners in Colorado, defying the power and wealth of the Rockefellers. The I.W.W. was born—revolutionary, militant, demanding "one big union" for everyone, skilled and unskilled, black and white, men and women, native-born and foreign-born.

Over a million people read the "Appeal to Reason" and other socialist newspapers. In proportion to population, it would be as if today, over three million Americans read a socialist press. The party had 100,000 members, and twelve hundred office-holders in 340 municipalities. Socialism was especially strong in the Southwest, among tenant farmers, railroad workers, coal miners, lumberjacks. Oklahoma, home of the fiery Kate Richards O'Hare (jailed for opposing the war, she hurled a book through a skylight to bring fresh air into the foul-smelling jail block, bringing cheers from her fellow inmates) had 12,000 dues paying members in 1914 and over a hundred socialists in local offices.

The point of recalling all this is to remind us of the powerful appeal of the socialist idea to people alienated from the political system and aware of the growing stark disparities in income and wealth—as so many Americans are today. The word itself—"socialism"—may still carry the distortions of recent experience in bad places usurping the name. But anyone who goes around the country, or reads carefully the public opinion surveys over the past decade, can see that huge numbers of Americans agree on what should be the fundamental elements of a decent society: guaranteed food, housing, medical care for everyone; bread and butter as better guarantees of "national security" than guns and bombs, democratic control of corporate power, equal rights for all races, genders and sexual orientations, a recognition of the rights of immigrants as the unrecognized counterparts of our parents and grandparents,, the rejection of war and violence as solutions for tyranny and injustice.

There are people fearful of the word, all along the political spectrum. What is important, I think, is not the word, but a determination to hold up before a troubled public those ideas which are both bold and inviting, the more bold the more inviting. That's what the remembering of Debs and the socialist idea can do for us.

24

Discovering John Reed

The appearance in 1981 of a Hollywood movie, *Reds,* in which the main character is a Communist, the journalist John Reed, and is sympathetically portrayed, was startling. It was one of many pieces of evidence that the nation had moved a critical distance away from the Communist hysteria of the Fifties. The editors of the *Boston Globe* asked me, as a historian, to tell their readers about John Reed, and this piece appeared January 5, 1982.

Radicals are doubly exasperating. They not only refuse to conform to ideas of what true American patriots are like; they may not even fit common notions of what radicals are like. So with John Reed and Louise Bryant, who confounded and infuriated the guardians of cultural and political orthodoxy around the time of World War I. They are now being portrayed in Warren Beatty's grand movie, *Reds,* causing some critics to grumble about "communist chic" and "mod Marxism," in an unwitting replay of the barbs thrust at Reed and Bryant in their time.

It was bad enough that they and their remarkable friends—Max Eastman, Emma Goldman, Lincoln Steffens, Margaret Sanger—spoke out for sexual freedom in a country dominated by Christian righteousness, or opposed militarization in a time of jingoism and war, or advocated socialism when business and government were clubbing and shooting strikers, or welcomed what seemed to them the first proletarian revolution in history.

What was worse was that they refused to remain mere writers and intellectuals, assailing the system with words; they walked picket lines, loved freely, defied government committees, went to jail. They declared for revolution in their actions as well as their art, ignoring those cautions against commitment offered, in any generation, by the voyeurs of social movements.

John Reed could not be forgiven by the Establishment (nor even by some of its critics, like Walter Lippmann and Eugene O'Neill) for refusing to separate art and insurgency, for being not only rebellious in his prose but imaginative in his activism. He saw revolt as not mere fulmination, but fun, not just analysis but adventure. This caused some of his liberal friends to take him less seriously (Lippmann spoke of his "inordinate desire to be arrested"), not understanding that, to the power elite of the country, protest joined to imagination was dangerous, courage combined with wit was no joke. Grim rebels can be jailed, but the highest treason, for which there is no adequate punishment, is to make rebellion attractive.

Jack Reed, his friends called him. He was a poet all his life, from his comfortable childhood in Portland, Oregon, through Harvard College, peasant uprisings in Mexico, the strikes of silkworkers in New Jersey and coal miners in Colorado, the war fronts of Europe, the shouting, singing crowds of the Bolshevik revolution in Petrograd. But as his fellow editor of the *Masses*, Max Eastman, wrote: "Poetry to Reed was not only a matter of writing words but of living life." His many poems, in fact, were not memorable, but he rushed into the center of wars and revolutions, strikes and demonstrations, with the eye of a movie camera, before there was one, and the memory of a tape recorder, before that existed. He made history come alive for the readers of popular magazines and impoverished radical monthlies.

At Harvard between 1906 and 1910, Reed was an athlete (swimming and water polo), a prankster, a cheer leader, a writer for the *Lampoon*, a student of the famous writing teacher they called Copey (Charles Townsend Copeland), at the same time, a protégé of the muckraker Lincoln Steffens. He was a mischievous critic of Harvard snobbery, though not a member of Walter Lippmann's Socialist Club. On graduation, he worked his way aboard a freighter to Europe—London, Paris, Madrid—then returned to join a cluster of Bohemian-radical writers living in Greenwich Village, where Steffens helped him get his first job doing rather routine editorial work for a literary political magazine called the *American*.

In New York in 1912, for anyone who looked around as sharply as John Reed, the contrasts of wealth and poverty stunned the senses. He began writing for the *Masses*, a new magazine edited by Max Eastman (brother of the socialist-feminist Crystal Eastman) and penned a manifesto: "Poems, stories, and drawings, rejected by the capitalist press on account of their excellence, will find a welcome in this magazine." The *Masses* was alive, not a party organ, but a party, with anarchists and socialists, artists and writers, and undefinable rebels of all sorts in its pages: Carl Sandburg and Amy Lowell, William Carlos Williams, Upton Sinclair. And from abroad, Bertrand Russell, Gorky, Picasso.

The times trembled with class struggle. Reed went to Lawrence, Massachusetts, where women and children had walked out of the textile mills and were carrying on a heartrending, heroic strike with the help of the IWW (the revolutionary Industrial Workers of the World) and the Socialist Party. Reed met Bill Haywood, the IWW leader (in one description, "a great battered hulk of a man, with one eye gone, and an eminent look in the other"). From Haywood he learned of the strike of 25,000 silk workers across the Hudson River in Paterson, asking for an eight-hour day and being clubbed by the police. The press was not reporting any of this, so Reed went to Paterson. It was not in him to stand off and take notes. He walked the picket line, was arrested for refusing to move on, spent four days in jail.

When he wrote about this for the *Masses*, it was a new writing for him—angry, involved. He attended a mass meeting for the Paterson strikers, heard the young Irish radical Elizabeth Gurley Flynn speak of the power of folded arms, and Reed himself—never shy—led the crowd in singing the *Marseillaise* and the *Internationale*. He and Mabel Dodge, whose Fifth Avenue apartment was a center for art and politics (and who was soon to become his lover) got a wild, brilliant idea—to do a pageant on the strike in Madison Square Garden, with a thousand workers in the cast. Reed worked day and night on the script; the scenery was painted by John Sloan; and 15,000 people came and cheered.

In Mexico in 1914, Pancho Villa was leading a rebellion of peasants, and the *Metropolitan* asked Reed to go as its correspondent. Reed was soon in the thick of the Mexican Revolution, riding with Villa himself, sending back stories which were acclaimed by Walter Lippmann as "the finest reporting that's ever been done.... The variety of his impressions, the resources and color of his language seemed inexhaustible...and Villa's revolution, till then reported only as a nuisance, began to unfold itself into throngs of moving people in a gorgeous panorama of earth and sky." Reed's collection of articles, *Insurgent Mexico*, was not what is admired in journalism schools as "objective reporting." It was meant to help a revolution.

Reed had barely returned to New York, acclaimed now as a great journalist, when the shocking news of the Ludlow Massacre spread through the country. In Southern Colorado, striking miners had been machine-gunned and their families burned to death, attacked by National Guardsmen in the pay of the Rockefellers. He was soon on the scene, writing "The Colorado War."

Summer, 1914, he was in Provincetown, which was to become his refuge those next years, for swimming, writing, love-making (until 1916, a stormy affair with Mabel Dodge). That August, the war began in Europe. In an unpublished manuscript, Reed wrote: "And here are the nations, flying at each other's throats like dogs...and art, industry, commerce, individual liberty, life itself taxed to maintain monstrous machines of death."

Reed went home to Portland to see his mother, who never approved of his radical ideas. There, at the local IWW hall, he heard Emma Goldman speak. It was an experience. She was that generation's powerhouse of feminism and anarchism, her life itself proof that one could be a joyful, serious revolutionary.

The big periodicals of New York pressed him to cover the European war for them, and he agreed to go for the *Metropolitan*. At the same time he wrote an article for the *Masses*. It was a war for profit, he said. On the way to Europe, he was conscious of the rich on the first-class decks, and three thousand Italians kept like animals in the hold. He was soon in England, in Switzerland and Germany, and then, in France, walking through the fields of war: rain, mud, corpses. What depressed him most was the murderous patriotism seizing everyone on both sides, even some Socialists, like H.G. Wells in England.

When he returned to the States after four months, he found the radicals Upton Sinclair and John Dewey among the patriots. And Walter Lippmann too. Lippmann, now editor of the *New Republic*, wrote in December, 1914 a curious essay: "The Legendary John

Reed." It defined the distance between himself and Reed. "By temperament he is not a professional writer or reporter. He is a person who enjoys himself." And then Lippmann, who clearly had pride in himself as "a professional writer," gave the ultimate dismissal: "Reed has no detachment and is proud of it."

It was true. Reed went back to the war in 1915, this time to Russia, to the burned and looted villages, to the mass killings of the Jews by the Tsar's soldiers, to Bucharest, Constantinople, Sofia, then Serbia and Greece. It was clear to him what patriotism meant: death by machine-gun fire or by famine, by smallpox, diphtheria, cholera, typhus. Back in America, he listened to the endless talk about military preparedness against "the enemy," and wrote for the *Masses* that the enemy for the American working man was the 2 percent of the population which owned 60 percent of the national wealth. "We advocate that the workingman prepare to defend himself against that enemy. This is our Preparedness."

Early in 1916, John Reed met Louise Bryant in Portland and they fell immediately in love. She left her husband and joined Reed in New York. It was the start of a passionate, poetic relationship. She was herself a writer and an anarchist of sorts. That summer Reed sought respite from the sounds of war on Provincetown's quiet beaches, with Bryant. There is a snapshot of her lying on the sands, nude and demure.

By April 1917, Woodrow Wilson was asking Congress to declare war on Germany, and John Reed wrote in the *Masses*. "War means an ugly mob-madness, crucifying the truth-tellers, choking the artists.... It is not our war." He testified before Congress against conscription: "I do not believe in this war...I would not serve in it."

When Emma Goldman and Alexander Berkman were arrested under the Draft Act for "conspiracy to induce persons not to register," Reed was a witness in their defense. They were convicted and sent to prison. So were a thousand other Americans who opposed the war. Radical newspapers were banned, among them the *Masses*.

Reed was distressed by the way the working classes in Europe and America were supporting the war and forgetting the class struggle. Yet he continued to hope: "I cannot give up the idea that out of democracy will be born the new world—richer, braver, freer, more beautiful."

From Russia in 1917 came thunderous news. The Tsar, the old regime, were overthrown. A revolution was in progress. Here at last, Reed thought, was an entire population which refused to go on with the slaughter, turned on its own ruling class, and was setting about the creation of a new society, its outlines not yet clear, but its spirit intoxicating.

With Louise Bryant, he set sail for Finland and Petrograd. The revolution was bursting all around them, and they immersed themselves in its excitement: the mass meetings, the workers taking over factories, the soldiers declaring their opposition to the war, the Petrograd Soviet electing a Bolshevik majority. Then, on November 6 and 7, the swift, bloodless take-over of the railroad stations, telegraph, telephone, post office. And finally, workers and soldiers rushing ecstatically into the Winter Palace.

Racing from scene to scene, Reed took notes with incredible speed, gathered up every leaflet, poster and proclamation, and then, in early 1918, went back to the United States to write his story. On arrival, his notes were confiscated. He found himself under indictment with other editors of the *Masses* for opposing the war, but at the trial, where he and Eastman testified eloquently, boldly, about their beliefs, the jury could not reach a decision and the charges were dropped.

Now Reed was everywhere in the country, lecturing on the war, the Russian Revolution. At Tremont Temple in Boston he was heckled by Harvard students. In Indiana he met Eugene Debs, who would soon be sentenced to ten years for speaking against the war. In Chicago he attended the trial of Bill Haywood and a hundred other IWW leaders, who would get long prison sentences. That September, after he spoke to a rally of four thousand people, Reed was arrested for discouraging recruitment in the armed forces.

He finally got his Russian notes back, and in two months of furious writing produced *Ten Days That Shook the World.* It became the classic eyewitness account of the Bolshevik Revolution, its words swarming over the pages with the sounds, as it seemed then, of a new world being born: "Up the Nevsky, in the sour twilight, crowds were battling for the latest papers.... On every corner, in every open space, thick groups were clustered; arguing soldiers and students...The Petrograd Soviet was meeting continuously at Smolny, a centre of storm, delegates falling down asleep on the floor and rising again to take part in the debate, Trotsky, Kamenev, Volodarsky speaking six, eight, twelve hours a day..."

In 1919, the war was over, but Allied armies had invaded Russia, and the hysteria continued in the United States. The country that had made the word "revolution" glorious throughout the world now was frightened of it. Non-citizens were rounded up by the thousands, arrested, deported without trial. There were strikes all over the country, and clashes with police. Reed became involved in the formation of the Communist Workers Party, went to Russia as a delegate to the meetings of the Communist International. There he argued with party bureaucrats, wondered what was happening with the revolution, met Emma Goldman in Moscow, and listened to her cry out her disillusionment.

He continued to hope. He rushed from meeting to meeting, from a conference in Moscow to a mass meeting of Asians on the Black Sea. He was wearing himself out, and he fell sick, feverish, delirious. It was typhus. At thirty-three, in a Moscow hospital, at the height of his love affair with his wife and comrade Louise Bryant, and with the idea of revolution, he died.

John Reed's body was buried near the Kremlin wall as a hero. But in truth, his soul does not belong to any Establishment, there or here or anywhere. Strangely, in the year 1981, sixty years after his death, millions of Americans will learn of John Reed because of a motion picture. If even a tiny fraction of these are led thereby to think about war and injustice, art and commitment, about enlarging friendship beyond national boundaries for the possibility of a better world, that is a huge accomplishment for one brief, intensely-lived life.

25

Jack London's
The Iron Heel

I first encountered Jack London as a writer of adventure stories, when I was a teen-ager. After I became interested in political ideas, and learned that he was a Socialist and that he had written a political novel, *The Iron Heel*, I rushed to read it. Years later I was asked to write an introduction to a new edition of the book (Bantam, 1971), and this gave me an opportunity to review Jack London's life and to read the book once more.

J ack London climbed, sailed, stormed through forty years of life, all ending in the torment of sickness, and the calculated swallowing of a large dose of morphine tablets. Tired, he lowered himself into death, like the hero of his autobiographical novel, *Martin Eden*.

He had come out of the slums of San Francisco, the child of an unwed woman who held seances, and whose lover, a scholarly lecturer on astrology, denied he had fathered her son. By the time he was fifteen he had been a newsboy, worked in a cannery, begun to read hungrily the books of the Oakland Public Library, become a sailor and a fisherman, found a mistress, and was drinking heavily.

Before he was twenty-one, he had worked in a jute mill and laundry, hoboed the railroads to the East Coast, been clubbed by a policeman on the streets of New York, been arrested for vagrancy in Niagara Falls, watched men beaten and tortured in jail, joined the Socialist Party, pirated oysters in San Francisco Bay, read Flaubert, Tolstoy, Melville, and the Communist Manifesto, shot rapids and climbed mountains in the Klondike gold rush, preached socialism in the Alaskan gold camps in the winter of 1896, sailed 2,000 miles back through the Bering Sea, and sold his first adventure stories to magazines.

At thirty-one, he had written twenty books, married twice, run for mayor of Oakland on the Socialist ticket, covered the Russo-Japanese War, sailed to Hawaii and Polynesia, made huge sums of money, and spent every dollar. The books and stories that made him world-famous were of the sea, of dogs, of men in loving combat with the wilderness, the snows, the night.

Around 1906, Jack London set out on his great socialist novel, *The Iron Heel.* Also at this time, he wrote about his own past: "I was in the pit, the abyss, the human cesspool, the shambles and charnelhouse of our civilization...I shall say only that the things I saw there gave me a terrible scare."

That terror, along with the vision of a socialist world and the brotherhood of man, he poured into the fantasy-realism of *The Iron Heel.* The imagination that had led people everywhere to devour his adventure stories now produced bizarre political conjurings: The First and Second Revolts, the Chicago Commune, The Mercenaries and the Frisco Reds, the Philomaths and the Valkyries, the Oligarchy, and the People of the Abyss.

If we take *The Iron Heel* as a premonition of the future—to bemuse us, fascinate us, frighten us—we will be deceived. It is the *present* that haunts a serious spinner of futuristic tales, and so it did Jack London. He uses the future to entice us out of the constricting corridors of here and now, far enough so that we can look back and see more clearly what is happening. He uses the love of Avis Cunningham for the remarkable Ernest Everhard to draw us into empathy with an undeniably arrogant but also undeniably attractive man who leads a socialist revolution in the United States.

But is Jack London's present also ours? Can the things he said about the United States in 1906 be applied to the nation in 1970? Have we not put behind us the wrongs of that older time, buried them under an avalanche of reforms and affluence? Have we not become a welfare state at home, a fearless defender of freedom abroad? In the Fifties, many Americans thought so.

At the start of the Seventies, however, there is a new mood. A fresh generation (of *radicals*, we begin to say, but there are too many of them to fit such a narrow definition) seems to have reached the conclusion that, aside from frills, tokens, gadgets, and rhetoric, all of which have proliferated in this century, the United States has not changed its basic characteristics: the rule of corporate wealth, the use of the big stick to bludgeon the discontented, both at home and abroad.

A formidable number of young people have lost their respect for the system, not because of books and lectures, but by observation and experience. As tiny children, they crawled under desks while sirens wailed in a preview of the atomic destruction of the earth. It seems now that they probably knew, with an intelligence far greater than that of teachers or parents or the country's leaders, how absurd it was to seek shelter under a wooden desk from the madness of governments armed with hydrogen bombs. By the time they grew up enough to read *Catch-22*, Yossarian's words shattered the cold war demonology of "them" and "us" and spoke to their childish wisdom: "The enemy is anybody who is going to get you killed, no matter which side he's on."

This generation watched on television as blacks were beaten bloody by Southern policemen while the FBI, sworn to uphold "law and order," stood by taking notes. They watched while blacks stealing shoes from store windows were shot dead by Northern policemen, who were then exonerated by the courts. In their living rooms they saw American soldiers ravage Vietnamese villages, bombing, shooting, setting fire to ancestral homes, laying waste an entire country, all in the name of freedom and peace. They saw the leaders of the country hurling the bodies of thousands of Americans into the Asian pyre in a lust of national righteousness.

And when these same young people went out onto the streets and campuses to protest, they too were clubbed, and some were killed, all in the name of stopping "violence." The America of 1970 is, perhaps, more shrewd at covering its deeds with slogans, than was the America of 1906. But the iron heel comes down as before.

In Jack London's time (1914), National Guardsmen fired into the tents of striking miners at Ludlow, Colorado, and killed twenty-five of them. In the spring of 1970, National Guardsmen fired into a crowd of striking students in Ohio and killed four of them. The killing in Colorado was justified by John D. Rockefeller, Jr., who owned the coal mines there, as the defense of "a great principle": the right to work in the mines. The killing in Ohio half a century later was justified also in the name of a principle: "law and order." No National Guardsmen were indicted in Colorado in 1914, but a strike leader was. No National Guardsmen were indicted in Ohio in 1970, but twenty-five demonstrators were.

In Jack London's time (1917, East St. Louis), a mob of civilians killed black men and women while the national government watched, claiming lack of jurisdiction. In our time (1964, Mississippi), two white and one black civil rights workers were killed by a mob including local law enforcement officers, while the national government stood by, claiming lack of jurisdiction.

Even those who live comfortably today in America live uncomfortably, on the crater's edge of violence: war, prisons, ghettos. The greatest violence comes not from protesters and revolutionaries but from governments. The greatest lawlessness is that of "law and order." Despite the tinsel of wealth and "progress" on all sides, what the workingman Ernest Everhard told the professor's daughter Avis Cunningham remains true: "Our boasted civilization is based upon blood, soaked in blood, and neither you nor I nor any of us can escape the scarlet stains."

The footnotes of *The Iron Heel*, supposedly written many centuries later to inform readers of what life was like in the early twentieth century, still cut deep to fundamental truths: "In those days, thievery was incredibly prevalent. Everybody stole property from everybody else. The lords of society stole legally, or else legalized their stealing, while the poorer classes stole illegally." In the America of 1970, petty thieves fill the jails-but Congress and the President approve tax legislation enabling the oil companies to legally steal millions of dollars from the public.

The corporation lawyer speaks bluntly to Avis: "What's right got to do with it? You see all those books. All my reading and studying of them has taught me that law is one thing and right is another thing." And Avis' words to him might be addressed today to that whole army of professionals trained by a complex society: "Tell me, when one surrenders his personal feelings to his professional feelings, may not the action be defined as a sort of spiritual mayhem?"

Since Jack London's time, women have been given the right to vote, the election of senators has been transferred from the state legislatures to the public, and millions of blacks have joined the voting rolls. But the terse footnote in Chapter 5 of *The Iron Heel* still has the sound of truth: "Even as late as 1912 AD, the great mass of the people still persisted in the belief that they ruled the country by virtue of their ballots. In reality, the country was ruled by what were called political machines."

Jack London's ultimate criticism of the capitalism of his day remains authentic: "In the face of the facts that modern man lives more wretchedly than the cave-man, and that his producing power is a thousand times greater than that of the cave-man, no other conclusion is possible than that the capitalist class has mismanaged...criminally and selfishly mismanaged." Perhaps the comparison with the cave-man is not too absurd, considering what proportion of the world is still sick, hungry, miserable, bombed-out; and how even the middle classes are trapped in an environment of polluted air, poisoned water, adulterated food, walled-off communities, unsatisfying jobs, adding up to both psychic and material insecurity. With our enormous wealth in the United States we have built highways, motor cars, motels, office buildings, guns, bombs, planes; we have wasted our resources on things either nonessential or dangerous, when these great resources—rationally, humanely used—could make life warm and human for all. London's point still holds: the profit of corporations, not the needs of people, decides what is done with the country's natural wealth.

Still fresh in the memory of 1906 was the take-over of the Philippines by the U.S. Army, all in the name of saving them from someone else's control, and the crushing of the Filipino rebels who opposed the American occupation. Someone says to Ernest Everhard in a passage remarkably prophetic for Vietnam: "Why, you spoke of sending the militia to the Philippines. That is unconstitutional. The Constitution especially states that the militia cannot be sent out of the country." And he replies: "What's the Constitution got to do with it?"

In the Fifties, the consciousness of the brutality of Stalin's socialism was so acute and the memory of Naziism so bitter, as to make *The Iron Heel* seem more a commentary on those two societies than on what seemed the more benign, if flawed, American system. Today, we are more aware that *all* powerful states, including the United States, waste the resources of their countrymen, prey on smaller nations, use "law and order" to maintain power and privilege, and crush the dissenting few while pacifying the majority with promises, slogans, and symbols of progress.

Yet, with all these remarkable perceptions, *The Iron Heel* stopped short of understanding certain things which we, a half century later, can see a bit more clearly. Jack London's vision is still inviting: "Let us not destroy those wonderful machines that produce efficiently and cheaply. Let us control them. Let us profit by their efficiency and cheapness. Let us run them for ourselves. That, gentlemen, is socialism..."

We know now that this prescription is not enough, if the "us" becomes a bureaucratic party substituting for the capitalist state. We will have to develop an "us" in which the control of the machinery is local, held by the people who work at it, and yet where all who are affected by the production—the consumer, other producers—have ways of expressing their desires. To establish cooperative control of production, combining the advantages of centralized efficiency with local controls in a complex, technologically advanced society, is an art demanding thought and experimentation.

We suspect now, too, that Jack London's prescription for change—an armed revolution—which seemed so natural in 1906, is inadequate, given such sophisticated controls as we have today in the United States. London swung swiftly from faith in the ballot box, which many Socialists of his day shared, to disillusionment with that and belief in armed rebellion. Thus, Ernest Everhard rushes from one to the other: "And in the day that we sweep to victory at the ballot-box, and you refuse to turn over to us the government we have constitutionally and peacefully captured, and you demand what we are going to do about it—in that day, I say, we shall answer you; and in roar of shell and shrapnel and in whine of machine guns shall our answer be couched."

In the modern, powerful, industrial state both these tactics—voting and armed insurrection—are decoys. The ballot box, a tawdry token of democracy, enables shrewd, effective control in the mass society, by those on top. And armed revolution is so clearly suicidal against the power of the great national state, that we must suspect its advocates of being police agents—as in the abortive uprisings in *The Iron Heel.*

There is another emerging truth which Jack London ignored, to which this generation is especially sensitive: that the mode of revolution helps determine its future course. A "revolution" accomplished by the ballot box perpetuates the notion that real change can come about by manipulating papers, rather than by people struggling to change their personal lives, their immediate relationships, their communities, their work. Revolutions by force of arms carry forward into the new society that ruthlessness which London himself depicts, and too readily accepts, in *The Iron Heel.* Perhaps we have learned enough in the past half century to begin to think of a novel approach to revolution.

A new mode of revolution would go far beyond the ballot box. People everywhere would begin to live cooperatively, not in mass organizations which override individual feelings, but in small groups based on working together, resisting the state together. In such groups, new relationships of intimacy and cooperation, born of common struggles, could develop between black and white, male and female, old and young. All this, in the midst of an inhuman society, while fighting to change that society.

People would work as cultural and political guerrillas, mobile, imaginative, so embedded in the lower structures of the society, and in its crevices, in so many places, as to be invulnerable to the crude, massed power of the state. If crushed in one place, these affinity groups would rise again in ten other places, until there were so many changed minds, so many changed ways of living, that the revolution would not be defeated because it would be already here. The old structures, despite their wealth and arms, would flail ineffectually at such a revolution, and then begin to wither, because their sustenance—the labor that operates them, the minds that accept them—had turned to other things.

At the least, Jack London's *The Iron Heel* may cause us to think, not about some time long past, or some fantasy far ahead, but about now, here, ourselves.

Suggestions
for Further
Reading

Some suggestions for further reading on history. I am not giving a formal listing of publishers, dates, and places because
public libraries can easily locate books by title and/or author.

I had not thought much about the social role of the historian until I
read Robert Lynd's *Knowledge for What?* Alfred North Whitehead's
The Aims of Education explores such questions too. Another thoughtful
book about the problems of writing history (objectivity, morality, science,
etc.) is the book by the British historian E.H. Carr, *What is History?*

In the early 20th century, an American writer, James Harvey
Robinson, wrote a provocative book on this subject, *The New History*.
There is an excellent collection of essays by Hans Meyerhoff, *The
Philosophy of History in Our Time*. And a superb book by Peter Novick on
the issue of objectivity among historians, *That Noble Dream*.

In the Sixties, Jesse Lemisch, a young radical historian, wrote a biting critique of the historical profession: *On Active Service in War and
Peace*. There are certain historians who represent for me the ideal joining
of impeccable research and social conscience. One is the British historian E.P. Thompson, who wrote *The Making of the English Working Class*.
Another is an American, Richard Drinnon, as in his brilliant book about
American expansionism, *Facing West*.

Also by Howard Zinn:

LaGuardia in Congress (Cornell University Press, 1959)

The Southern Mystique (Alfred Knopf, 1964)

SNCC: The New Abolitionists (Beacon Press, 1964)

New Deal Thought, ed. (Bobbs Merrill, 1965)

Vietnam: The Logic of Withdrawal (Beacon Press, 1967)

Disobedience and Democracy (Random House, 1968)

The Politics of History (Beacon Press, 1970)

The Pentagon Papers: Critical Essays, ed. with Noam Chomsky (Beacon Press, 1972)

Postwar America (Bobbs Merrill, 1973)

Justice in Everyday Life, ed. (William Morrow, 1974)

A People's History of the United States (Harper & Row, 1980)

The Twentieth Century: A People's History (HarperCollins, 1984)

Declarations of Independence: Cross-Examining American Ideology (HarperCollins, 1990)

Failure to Quit: Reflections of an Optimistic Historian (Common Courage Press, 1993)

You Can't Be Neutral on a Moving Train (Beacon Press, 1994)

The Zinn Reader (Seven Stories, 1997)

Howard Zinn on War (Seven Stories, 2001)

HOWARD ZINN grew up in the immigrant slums of Brooklyn, where he worked in shipyards in his late teens. He saw combat duty as an air force bombardier in World War II, and afterward received his doctorate in history from Columbia University. His first book, *La Guardia in Congress,* was an Albert Berveridge Prize winner. In 1956, he moved with his wife and children to Atlanta to become chairman of the history department of Spelman College. He has since written and edited many more books, including *A People's History of the United States; SNCC: The New Abolitionist; Disobedience and Democracy; The Politics of History; The Pentagon Papers: Critical Essays; You Can't Be Neutral on a Moving Train: A Personal History of Our Times;* and *The Zinn Reader.*

Zinn is also the author of three plays: *Emma, Daughter of Venus,* and *Marx in Soho.* Among the many honors Zinn has received, the most recent is the 1998 Lannan Literary Award for nonfiction. A professor emeritus of political science at Boston University, he lives with his wife, Roslyn, in the Boston area, near their children and grandchildren.